The Quintessence of Ibsenism

G. Bernard Shaw

BIBLIOLIFE

Copyright © BiblioLife, LLC

BiblioLife Reproduction Series: Our goal at BiblioLife is to help readers, educators and researchers by bringing back in print hard-to-find original publications at a reasonable price and, at the same time, preserve the legacy of literary history. The following book represents an authentic reproduction of the text as printed by the original publisher and may contain prior copyright references. While we have attempted to accurately maintain the integrity of the original work(s), from time to time there are problems with the original book scan that may result in minor errors in the reproduction, including imperfections such as missing and blurred pages, poor pictures, markings and other reproduction issues beyond our control. Because this work is culturally important, we have made it available as a part of our commitment to protecting, preserving and promoting the world's literature.

All of our books are in the "public domain" and some are derived from Open Source projects dedicated to digitizing historic literature. We believe that when we undertake the difficult task of re-creating them as attractive, readable and affordable books, we further the mutual goal of sharing these works with a larger audience. A portion of BiblioLife profits go back to Open Source projects in the form of a donation to the groups that do this important work around the world. If you would like to make a donation to these worthy Open Source projects, or would just like to get more information about these important initiatives, please visit www.bibliolife.com/opensource.

THE QUINTESSENCE OF IBSENISM: BY G. BERNARD SHAW.

LONDON: WALTER SCOTT
24 WARWICK LANE. 1891

CONTENTS.

		PAGE
I.	THE TWO PIONEERS	1
II.	IDEALS AND IDEALISTS	19
III.	THE WOMANLY WOMAN	31
IV.	THE PLAYS	46
	Brand	46
	Peer Gynt	49
	Emperor and Galilean	56
	The League of Youth	73
	Pillars of Society	75
	A Doll's House	78
	Ghosts	82
	An Enemy of the People	92
	The Wild Duck	96
	Rosmersholm	100
	The Lady from the Sea	109
	Hedda Gabler	112
V	THE MORAL OF THE PLAYS	122

APPENDIX 135

PREFACE.

IN the spring of 1890, the Fabian Society, finding itself at a loss for a course of lectures to occupy its summer meetings, was compelled to make shift with a series of papers put forward under the general heading "Socialism in Contemporary Literature" The Fabian Essayists, strongly pressed to do "something or other," for the most part shook their heads; but in the end Sydney Olivier consented to "take Zola"; I consented to "take Ibsen"; and Hubert Bland undertook to read all the Socialist novels of the day, an enterprise the desperate failure of which resulted in the most amusing paper of the series. William Morris, asked to read a paper on himself, flatly declined, but gave us one on Gothic Architecture. Stepniak also came to the rescue with a lecture on modern Russian fiction; and so the Society tided over the summer without having to close its doors, but also without having added anything whatever to the general stock of information on Socialism in Contemporary Literature. After this I cannot claim that my paper on Ibsen, which was duly read at the St James's Restaurant on the 18th July 1890, under the presidency of Mrs Annie Besant, and which was the first form of this little book, is an original work in the sense of being the result of a spontaneous internal impulse on my part. Having purposely couched it in the most provocative terms (of which traces may be found by the curious in its present state), I did not attach much importance to the somewhat lively debate that arose upon it; and I had laid it aside as a *pièce d'occasion* which had served its turn, when the production of *Rosmersholm* at the Vaudeville Theatre by Miss Farr, the inauguration of the Independent Theatre by Mr J. T. Grein with a performance of *Ghosts*, and the sensation created by the experiment of Miss Robins and Miss Lea with *Hedda Gabler*, started a frantic newspaper controversy, in which I could see no sign of any of the disputants having ever been forced by circumstances, as I had, to make up his mind definitely as to what Ibsen's plays meant, and to defend his view face to face with some of the

Preface.

keenest debaters in London. I allow due weight to the fact that Ibsen himself has not enjoyed this advantage (see page 56); but I have also shewn that the existence of a discoverable and perfectly definite thesis in a poet's work by no means depends on the completeness of his own intellectual consciousness of it. At any rate, the controversialists, whether in the abusive stage, or the apologetic stage, or the hero worshipping stage, by no means made clear what they were abusing, or apologizing for, or going into ecstasies about; and I came to the conclusion that my explanation might as well be placed in the field until a better could be found.

With this account of the origin of the book, and a reminder that it is not a critical essay on the poetic beauties of Ibsen, but simply an exposition of Ibsenism, I offer it to the public to make what they can of.

LONDON, *June* 1891.

THE QUINTESSENCE

OF

IBSENISM.

I.

THE TWO PIONEERS.

THAT is, pioneers of the march to the plains of heaven (so to speak).

The second, whose eyes are in the back of his head, is the man who declares that it is wrong to do something that no one has hitherto seen any harm in.

The first, whose eyes are very longsighted and in the usual place, is the man who declares that it is right to do something hitherto regarded as infamous.

The second is treated with great respect by the army. They give him testimonials; name him the Good Man; and hate him like the devil.

The first is stoned and shrieked at by the whole army. They call him all manner of opprobrious names; grudge him his bare bread and water; and secretly adore him as their saviour from utter despair.

Let me take an example from life of my pioneer. Shelley was a pioneer and nothing else: he did both first and second pioneer's work.

Now compare the effect produced by Shelley as abstinence preacher or second pioneer with that which he produced as indulgence preacher or first pioneer. For example:—

SECOND PIONEER PROPOSITION.—It is wrong to kill animals and eat them.

FIRST PIONEER PROPOSITION.—It is not wrong to take your sister as your wife.

Here the second pioneer appears as a gentle humanitarian, and the first as an unnatural corrupter of public morals and family life. So much easier is it to declare the right wrong than the wrong right in a society with a guilty conscience, to which, as to Dickens's detective, "Any possible move is a probable move provided it's in a wrong direction." Just as the liar's punishment is, not in the least that he is not believed, but that he cannot believe any one else, so a guilty society can more easily be persuaded that any apparently innocent act is guilty than that any apparently guilty act is innocent.

The English newspaper which best represents the guilty conscience of the middle class, or

The Two Pioneers.

dominant factor in society to-day, is the *Daily Telegraph*. If we can find the *Daily Telegraph* speaking of Ibsen as the *Quarterly Review* used to speak of Shelley, it will occur to us at once that there must be something of the first pioneer about Ibsen.

Mr Clement Scott, dramatic critic to the *Daily Telegraph*, a good-natured gentleman, not a pioneer, but emotional, impressionable, zealous, and sincere, accuses Ibsen of dramatic impotence, ludicrous amateurishness, nastiness, vulgarity, egotism, coarseness, absurdity, uninteresting verbosity, and suburbanity, declaring that he has taken ideas that would have inspired a great tragic poet, and vulgarized and debased them in dull, hateful, loathsome, horrible plays. This criticism, which occurs in a notice of the first performance of *Ghosts* in England, is to be found in the *Daily Telegraph* for the 14th March 1891, and is supplemented by a leading article which compares the play to an open drain, a loathsome sore unbandaged, a dirty act done publicly, or a lazar house with all its doors and windows open. Bestial, cynical, disgusting, poisonous, sickly, delirious, indecent, loathsome, fetid, literary carrion, crapulous stuff, clinical confessions: all these epithets are used in the article as descriptive of Ibsen's work. "Realism," says the writer, "is one thing; but the nostrils of the audience must not be visibly held before a play can be stamped as true to nature. It is difficult to expose in decorous words—the gross, and almost putrid indecorum of this play." As the performance of *Ghosts* took place on the evening of the 13th March, and the criticism appeared next morning, it is evident that Mr Scott must have gone straight from the theatre to the newspaper office, and there, in an almost hysterical condition, penned his share of this extraordinary protest. The literary workmanship bears marks of haste and disorder, which, however, only heighten the expression of the passionate horror produced in the writer by seeing *Ghosts* on the stage. He calls on the authorities to cancel the license of the theatre, and declares that he has been exhorted to laugh at honour, to disbelieve in love, to mock at virtue, to distrust friendship, and to deride fidelity. If this document were at all singular, it would rank as one of the curiosities of criticism, exhibiting, as it does, the most seasoned play-goer in the world thrown into convulsions by a performance which was witnessed with approval, and even with enthusiasm, by many persons of approved moral and artistic conscientiousness. But Mr Scott's criticism was hardly distinguishable in tone from hundreds of others which appeared simultaneously. His opinion was the vulgar opinion. Mr Alfred Watson, critic to the *Standard*, the leading Tory daily paper, proposed that proceedings should be taken against the theatre under Lord Campbell's Act for the suppression of disorderly houses. Clearly Mr Scott and his editor Sir Edwin Arnold, with whom rests the responsibility for the article which accompanied the criticism, may claim to represent a considerable party. How then is it that Ibsen, a Norwegian playwright of European celebrity, attracts one section of the English people so strongly that they hail him as the greatest living dramatic poet and moral teacher, whilst another section is so revolted by his works that they describe him in terms which they themselves admit are, by the necessities of the case, all but obscene? This phenomenon, which has occurred throughout Europe wherever Ibsen's plays have been acted, as well as in America and Australia, must be exhaustively explained before the plays can be described without danger of reproducing the same confusion in the reader's own mind. Such an explanation, therefore, must be my first business.

Understand, at the outset, that the explanation will not be an explaining away. Mr Clement Scott's judgment has not misled him in the least as to Ibsen's meaning. Ibsen means all that most revolts his critic. For example, in

Ghosts, the play in question, a clergyman and a married woman fall in love with one another. The woman proposes to abandon her husband and live with the clergyman. He recalls her to her duty, and makes her behave as a virtuous woman. She afterwards tells him that this was a crime on his part. Ibsen agrees with her, and has written the play to bring you round to his opinion. Mr Clement Scott does not agree with her, and believes that when you are brought round to her opinion you will be morally corrupted. By this conviction he is impelled to denounce Ibsen as he does, Ibsen being equally impelled to propagate the convictions which provoke the attack. Which of the two is right cannot be decided until it is ascertained whether a society of persons holding Ibsen's opinions would be higher or lower than a society holding Mr Clement Scott's.

There are many people who cannot conceive this as an open question. To them a denunciation of any of the recognized virtues is an incitement to unsocial conduct; and every utterance in which an assumption of the eternal validity of these virtues is not implicit, is a paradox. Yet all progress involves the beating of them from that position. By way of illustration, one may rake up the case of Proudhon, who nearly half a century ago denounced "property" as theft.

This was thought the very maddest paradox that ever man hazarded: it seemed obvious that a society which countenanced such a proposition would speedily be reduced to the condition of a sacked city. To-day schemes for the confiscation by taxation of mining royalties and ground rents are commonplaces of social reform; and the honesty of the relation of our big property holders to the rest of the community is challenged on all hands. It would be easy to multiply instances, though the most complete are now ineffective through the triumph of the original "paradox" having obliterated all memory of the opposition it first had to encounter. The point to seize is that social progress takes effect through the replacement of old institutions by new ones; and since every institution involves the recognition of the duty of conforming to it, progress must involve the repudiation of an established duty at every step. If the Englishman had not repudiated the duty of absolute obedience to his king, his political progress would have been impossible. If women had not repudiated the duty of absolute submission to their husbands, and defied public opinion as to the limits set by modesty to their education, they would never have gained the protection of the Married Women's Property Act or the power to qualify themselves as medical practitioners.

If Luther had not trampled on his duty to the head of his Church and on his vow of chastity, our priests would still have to choose between celibacy and profligacy. There is nothing new, then, in the defiance of duty by the reformer: every step of progress means a duty repudiated, and a scripture torn up. And every reformer is denounced accordingly, Luther as an apostate, Cromwell as a traitor, Mary Wollestonecraft as an unwomanly virago, Shelley as a libertine, and Ibsen as all the things enumerated in the *Daily Telegraph*.

This crablike progress of social evolution, in which the individual advances by seeming to go backward, continues to illude us in spite of all the lessons of history. To the pious man the newly made freethinker, suddenly renouncing supernatural revelation, and denying all obligation to believe the Bible and obey the commandments as such, appears to be claiming the right to rob and murder at large. But the freethinker soon finds reasons for not doing what he does not want to do; and these reasons seem to him to be far more binding on the conscience than the precepts of a book of which the divine inspiration cannot be rationally proved. The pious man is at last forced to admit—as he was in the case of the late Charles Bradlaugh, for instance —that the disciples of Voltaire and Tom Paine do not pick pockets or cut throats oftener than your even Christian: he actually is driven to doubt whether Voltaire himself really screamed and saw the devil on his deathbed.

This experience by no means saves the rationalist * from falling into the same conservatism when the time comes for his own belief to be questioned. No sooner has he triumphed over the theologian than he forthwith sets up as binding on all men the duty of acting logically with the object of securing the greatest good of the greatest number, with the result that he is presently landed in vivisection, Contagious Diseases Acts, dynamite conspiracies, and other grotesque but strictly reasonable abominations. Reason becomes Dagon, Moloch, and Jehovah rolled into one. Its devotees exult in having freed themselves from the old slavery to a collection of books written by Jewish men of letters. To worship such books was, they can prove, manifestly as absurd as to worship sonatas composed by German musicians, as was done by the hero of Wagner's novelette, who sat up on his deathbed to say his creed, beginning, " I believe in God, Mozart, and Beethoven." The Voltairian freethinker despises such a piece of

---

* I had better here warn students of philosophy that I am speaking of rationalism, not as classified in the books, but as apparent in men.

sentiment, but is it not much more sensible to worship a sonata constructed by a musician than to worship a syllogism constructed by a logician, since the sonata may at least inspire feelings of awe and devotion? This does not occur to the votary of reason; and rationalist "free-thinking" soon comes to mean syllogism worship with rites of human sacrifice; for just as the rationalist's pious predecessor thought that the man who scoffed at the Bible must infallibly yield without resistance to all his criminal propensities, so the rationalist in turn becomes convinced that when a man once loses his faith in Mr Herbert Spencer's *Data of Ethics*, he is no longer to be trusted to keep his hands off his neighbour's person, purse, or wife.

In process of time the age of reason had to go its way after the age of faith. In actual experience, the first shock to rationalism came from the observation that though nothing could persuade women to adopt it, their inaptitude for reasoning no more prevented them from arriving at right conclusions than the masculine aptitude for it saved men from arriving at wrong ones. When this generalization had to be modified in view of the fact that some women did at last begin to try their skill at ratiocination, reason was not re-established on the throne; because the result of Woman's reasoning was that she began to fall into all the errors which men are just learning to mistrust. From the moment she set about doing things for reasons instead of merely finding reasons for what she wanted to do, there was no saying what mischief she would be at next; since there are just as good reasons for burning a heretic at the stake as for rescuing a shipwrecked crew from drowning—in fact, there are better. One of the first and most famous utterances of rationalism would have condemned it without further hearing had its full significance been seen at the time. Voltaire, taking exception to the trash of some poetaster, was met with the plea "One must live." " I dont see the necessity," replied Voltaire. The evasion was worthy of the Father of Lies himself; for Voltaire was face to face with the very necessity he was denying—must have known, consciously or not, that it was the universal postulate —would have understood, if he had lived to-day, that since all human institutions are constructed to fulfil man's will, and that his will is to live even when his reason teaches him to die, logical necessity, which was the sort Voltaire meant (the other sort being visible enough) can never be a motor in human action, and is, in short, not necessity at all. But that was not brought to light in Voltaire's time; and he died impenitent, bequeathing to his disciples that most logical of agents, the guillotine, which also "did not see the necessity." In our own century the recognition of the will as distinct from the reasoning machinery began to spread. Schopenhauer was the first among the moderns [*] to appreciate the enormous practical importance of the distinction, and to make it clear to amateur metaphysicians by concrete instances. Out of his teaching came the formulation of the dilemma that Voltaire shut his eyes to. Here it is. Rationally considered, life is only worth living when its pleasures are greater than its

---

[*] I say the moderns, because the will is our old friend the soul or spirit of man; and the doctrine of justification, not by works, but by faith, clearly derives its validity from the consideration that no action, taken apart from the will behind it, has any moral character: for example, the acts which make the murderer and incendiary infamous are exactly similar to those which make the patriotic hero famous. "Original sin" is the will doing mischief. "Divine grace" is the will doing good. Our fathers, unversed in the Hegelian dialectic, could not conceive that these two, each the negation of the other, were the same. Schopenhauer's philosophy, like that of all pessimists, is really based on the old view of the will as original sin, and on the 1750-1850 view that the intellect is the divine grace that is to save us from it. It is as well to warn those who fancy that Schopenhauerism is one and indivisible, that acceptance of its metaphysics by no means involves endorsement of its philosophy.

pains. Now to a generation which has ceased to believe in heaven, and has not yet learned that the degradation by poverty of four out of every five of its number is artificial and remediable, the fact that life is not worth living is obvious. It is useless to pretend that the pessimism of Koheleth, Shakspere, Dryden, and Swift can be refuted if the world progresses solely by the destruction of the unfit, and yet can only maintain its civilization by manufacturing the unfit in swarms of which that appalling proportion of four to one represents but the comparatively fit survivors. Plainly then, the reasonable thing for the rationalists to do is to refuse to live But as none of them will commit suicide in obedience to this demonstration of "the necessity" for it, there is an end of the notion that we live for reasons instead of in fulfilment of our will to live. Thus we are landed afresh in mystery; for positive science gives no account whatever of this will to live. Indeed the utmost light that positive science throws is but feeble in comparison with the illumination that was looked forward to when it first began to dazzle us with its analyses of the machinery of sensation—its researches into the nature of sound and the construction of the ear, the nature of light and the construction of the eye, its measurement of the speed of sensation, its localization of the functions of the brain, and its hints as to the possibility of producing a homunculus presently as the fruit of its chemical investigation of protoplasm. The fact remains that when Darwin, Haeckel, Helmholtz, Young, and the rest, popularized here among the middle class by Tyndall and Huxley, and among the proletariat by the lectures of the National Secular Society, have taught you all they know, you are still as utterly at a loss to explain the fact of consciousness as you would have been in the days when you were satisfied with Chambers' *Vestiges of Creation*. Materialism, in short, only isolated the great mystery of consciousness by clearing away several petty mysteries with which we had confused it; just as rationalism isolated the great mystery of the will to live. The isolation made both more conspicuous than before. We thought we had escaped for ever from the cloudy region of metaphysics; and we were only carried further into the heart of them.*

---

* The correlation between rationalism and materialism in this process has some immediate practical importance. Those who give up materialism whilst clinging to rationalism generally either relapse into abject submission to the most paternal of the Churches, or are caught by the attempts, constantly renewed, of mystics to found a new faith by rationalizing on the hollowness of materialism. The hollowness has nothing in it; and if you have come to grief as a materialist by reasoning about something, you are not likely, as a mystic, to improve matters by reasoning about nothing

We have not yet worn off the strangeness of the position to which we have now been led. Only the other day our highest boast was that we were reasonable human beings. To-day we laugh at that conceit, and see ourselves as wilful creatures. Ability to reason accurately is as desirable as ever, since it is only by accurate reasoning that we can calculate our actions so as to do what we intend to do—that is, to fulfil our will; but faith in reason as a prime motor is no longer the criterion of the sound mind, any more than faith in the Bible is the criterion of righteous intention.

At this point, accordingly, the illusion as to the retrogressive movement of progress recurs as strongly as ever. Just as the beneficent step from theology to rationalism seems to the theologist a growth of impiety, does the step from rationalism to the recognition of the will as the prime motor strike the rationalist as a lapse of common sanity, so that to both theologist and rationalist progress at last appears alarming, threatening, hideous, because it seems to tend towards chaos. The deists Voltaire and Tom Paine were, to the divines of their day, predestined devils, tempting mankind hellward. To deists and divines alike Ferdinand Lassalle, the godless self-worshipper and man-worshipper would have been a monster. Yet many who to-day echo Lassalle's demand that economic and political institutions should be adapted to the poor man's will to eat and drink his fill out of the product of his own labour, are revolted by Ibsen's acceptance of the impulse towards greater freedom as sufficient ground for the repudiation of any customary duty, however sacred, that conflicts with it. Society—were it even as free as Lassalle's Social-Democratic republic—*must*, it seems to them, go to pieces when conduct is no longer regulated by inviolable covenants.

For what, during all these overthrowings of things sacred and things infallible, has been happening to that pre-eminently sanctified thing, Duty? Evidently it cannot have come off scatheless. First there was man's duty to God, with the priest as assessor. That was repudiated; and then came Man's duty to his neighbour, with Society as the assessor. Will this too be repudiated, and be succeeded by Man's duty to himself, assessed by himself? And if so, what will be the effect on the conception of Duty in the abstract? Let us see.

I have just called Lassalle a self-worshipper. In doing so I cast no reproach on him; for this is the last step in the evolution of the conception of duty. Duty arises at first, a gloomy tyranny, out of man's helplessness, his self-mistrust, in a word, his abstract fear. He

The Two Pioneers.

personifies all that he abstractly fears as God, and straightway becomes the slave of his duty to God. He imposes that slavery fiercely on his children, threatening them with hell, and punishing them for their attempts to be happy. When, becoming bolder, he ceases to fear everything, and dares to love something, this duty of his to what he fears evolves into a sense of duty to what he loves. Sometimes he again personifies what he loves as God; and the God of Wrath becomes the God of Love: sometimes he at once becomes a humanitarian, an altruist, acknowledging only his duty to his neighbour This stage is correlative to the rationalist stage in the evolution of philosophy and the capitalist phase in the evolution of industry. But in it the emancipated slave of God falls under the dominion of Society, which, having just reached a phase in which all the love is ground out of it by the competitive struggle for money, remorselessly crushes him until, in due course of the further growth of his spirit or will, a sense at last arises in him of his duty to himself. And when this sense is fully grown, which it hardly is yet, the tyranny of duty is broken ; for now the man's God is himself ; and he, self-satisfied at last, ceases to be selfish. The evangelist of this last step must therefore preach the repudiation of duty. This, to the unprepared of his generation, is indeed the wanton masterpiece of paradox. What! after all that has been said by men of noble life as to the secret of all right conduct being only "Duty, duty, duty," is he to be told now that duty is the primal curse from which we must redeem ourselves before we can advance another step on the road along which, as we imagine—having forgotten the repudiations made by our fathers —duty and duty alone has brought us thus far? But why not? God was once the most sacred of our conceptions; and he had to be denied. Then Reason became the Infallible Pope, only to be deposed in turn. Is Duty more sacred than God or Reason?

Having now arrived at the prospect of the repudiation of duty by Man, I shall make a digression on the subject of ideals and idealists, as treated by Ibsen. I shall go round in a loop, and come back to the same point by way of the repudiation of duty by Woman; and then at last I shall be in a position to describe the plays without risk of misunderstanding.

II.

IDEALS AND IDEALISTS.

WE have seen that as Man grows through the ages, he finds himself bolder by the growth of his spirit (if I may so name the unknown) and dares more and more to love and trust instead of to fear and fight. But his courage has other effects: he also raises himself from mere consciousness to knowledge by daring more and more to face facts and tell himself the truth. For in his infancy of helplessness and terror he could not face the inexorable; and facts being of all things the most inexorable, he masked all the threatening ones as fast as he discovered them; so that now every mask requires a hero to tear it off. The king of terrors, Death, was the Arch-Inexorable: Man could not bear the dread of that thought. He must persuade himself that Death could be propitiated, circumvented, abolished. How he fixed the mask of immortality on the face of Death for this purpose we all know. And he did the like with all disagreeables as long as they remained inevitable. Otherwise he must have gone mad with terror of the grim shapes around him, headed by the skeleton with the scythe and hourglass. The masks were his ideals, as he called them; and what, he would ask, would life be without ideals? Thus he became an idealist, and remained so until he dared to begin pulling the masks off and looking the spectres in the face—dared, that is, to be more and more a realist. But all men are not equally brave; and the greatest terror prevailed whenever some realist bolder than the rest laid hands on a mask which they did not yet dare to do without.

We have plenty of these masks around us still—some of them more fantastic than any of the Sandwich islanders' masks in the British Museum. In our novels and romances especially we see the most beautiful of all the masks—those devised to disguise the brutalities of the sexual instinct in the earlier stages of its development, and to soften the rigorous aspect of the iron laws by which Society regulates its gratification. When the social organism becomes bent on civilization, it has to force marriage and family life on the individual, because it can perpetuate itself in no other way whilst love is still known only by fitful glimpses, the basis of sexual relationship being in the main mere physical appetite. Under these circum-

stances men try to graft pleasure on necessity
by desperately pretending that the institution
forced upon them is a congenial one, making
it a point of public decency to assume always
that men spontaneously love their kindred better
than their chance acquaintances, and that the
woman once desired is always desired: also that
the family is woman's proper sphere, and that
no really womanly woman ever forms an attach-
ment, or even knows what it means, until she
is requested to do so by a man. Now if
anyone's childhood has been embittered by the
dislike of his mother and the ill-temper of his
father; if his wife has ceased to care for him
and he is heartily tired of his wife; if his brother
is going to law with him over the division
of the family property, and his son acting in
studied defiance of his plans and wishes, it is
hard for him to persuade himself that passion
is eternal and that blood is thicker than water.
Yet if he tells himself the truth, all his life seems
a waste and a failure by the light of it. It comes
then to this, that his neighbours must either
agree with him that the whole system is a mistake, and discard it for a new one, which cannot
possibly happen until social organization so far
outgrows the institution that Society can perpetuate itself without it; or else they must keep
him in countenance by resolutely making believe

that all the illusions with which it has been masked are realities.

For the sake of precision, let us imagine a community of a thousand persons, organized for the perpetuation of the species on the basis of the British family as we know it at present. Seven hundred of them, we will suppose, find the British family arrangement quite good enough for them. Two hundred and ninety-nine find it a failure, but must put up with it since they are in a minority. The remaining person occupies a position to be explained presently. The 299 failures will not have the courage to face the fact that they are failures—irremediable failures, since they cannot prevent the 700 satisfied ones from coercing them into conformity with the marriage law. They will accordingly try to persuade themselves that, whatever their own particular domestic arrangements may be, the family is a beautiful and holy natural institution. For the fox not only declares that the grapes he cannot get are sour: he also insists that the sloes he *can* get are sweet. Now observe what has happened. The family as it really is is a conventional arrangement, legally enforced, which the majority, because it happens to suit them, think good enough for the minority, whom it happens not to suit at all. The family as a beautiful and holy natural institution is only a fancy picture of what every family would have to be if everybody was to be suited, invented by the minority as a mask for the reality, which in its nakedness is intolerable to them. We call this sort of fancy picture an IDEAL; and the policy of forcing individuals to act on the assumption that all ideals are real, and to recognize and accept such action as standard moral conduct, absolutely valid under all circumstances, contrary conduct or any advocacy of it being discountenanced and punished as immoral, may therefore be described as the policy of IDEALISM. Our 299 domestic failures are therefore become idealists as to marriage; and in proclaiming the ideal in fiction, poetry, pulpit and platform oratory, and serious private conversation, they will far outdo the 700 who comfortably accept marriage as a matter of course, never dreaming of calling it an "institution," much less a holy and beautiful one, and being pretty plainly of opinion that idealism is a crackbrained fuss about nothing. The idealists, hurt by this, will retort by calling them Philistines. We then have our society classified as 700 Philistines and 299 idealists, leaving one man unclassified. He is the man who is strong enough to face the truth that the idealists are shirking. He says flatly of marriage, "This thing is a failure for many of us. It is insufferable that two human beings, having entered into relations which only warm affection can render tolerable, should be forced to maintain them after such affections have ceased to exist, or in spite of the fact that they have never arisen. The alleged natural attractions and repulsions upon which the family ideal is based do not exist; and it is historically false that the family was founded for the purpose of satisfying them. Let us provide otherwise for the social ends which the family subserves, and then abolish its compulsory character altogether." What will be the attitude of the rest to this outspoken man? The Philistines will simply think him mad. But the idealists will be terrified beyond measure at the proclamation of their hidden thought—at the presence of the traitor among the conspirators of silence—at the rending of the beautiful veil they and their poets have woven to hide the unbearable face of the truth. They will crucify him, burn him, violate their own ideals of family affection by taking his children away from him, ostracize him, brand him as immoral, profligate, filthy, and appeal against him to the despised Philistines, specially idealized for the occasion as SOCIETY. How far they will proceed against him depends on how far his courage exceeds theirs. At his worst, they call him cynic and paradoxer: at his best they do their utmost to ruin him if not to take his life. Thus, purblindly courageous moralists like Mandeville and Larochefoucauld, who merely state unpleasant facts without denying the validity of current ideals, and who indeed depend on those ideals to make their statements piquant, get off with nothing worse than this name of cynic, the free use of which is a familiar mark of the zealous idealist. But take the case of the man who has already served us as an example—Shelley. The idealists did not call Shelley a cynic: they called him a fiend until they invented a new illusion to enable them to enjoy the beauty of his lyrics—said illusion being nothing less than the pretence that since he was at bottom an idealist himself, his ideals must be identical with those of Tennyson and Longfellow, neither of whom ever wrote a line in which some highly respectable ideal was not implicit.*

---

* The following are examples of the two stages of Shelley criticism :—

"We feel as if one of the darkest of the fiends had been clothed with a human body to enable him to gratify his enmity against the human race, and as if the supernatural atrocity of his hate were only heightened by his power to do injury. So strongly has this impression dwelt upon our minds that we absolutely asked a friend, who had seen this individual, to describe him to us—as if a cloven hoof, or horn, or flames from the mouth, must have marked the external appearance of so bitter an enemy of mankind." (*Literary Gazette*, 19th May 1821.)

"A beautiful and ineffectual angel, beating in the void

Here the admission that Shelley, the realist, was an idealist too, seems to spoil the whole argument. And it certainly spoils its verbal consistency. For we unfortunately use this word ideal indifferently to denote both the institution which the ideal masks and the mask itself, thereby producing desperate confusion of thought, since the institution may be an effete and poisonous one, whilst the mask may be, and indeed generally is, an image of what we would fain have in its place. If the existing facts, with their masks on, are to be called ideals, and the future possibilities which the masks depict are also to be called ideals—if, again, the man who is defending existing institutions by maintaining their identity with their masks is to be confounded under one name with the man who is striving to realize the future possibilities by tearing the mask and the thing masked asunder, then the position cannot be intelligibly described by mortal pen: you and I, reader, will be at cross purposes at every sentence

---

his luminous wings in vain." (MATTHEW ARNOLD, in his preface to the selection of poems by Byron, dated 1881.)

The 1881 opinion is much sillier than the 1821 opinion. Further samples will be found in the articles of Henry Salt, one of the few writers on Shelley who understand his true position as a social pioneer.

Ideals and Idealists.

unless you allow me to distinguish pioneers like Shelley and Ibsen as realists from the idealists of my imaginary community of one thousand. If you ask why I have not allotted the terms the other way, and called Shelley and Ibsen idealists and the conventionalists realists, I reply that Ibsen himself, though he has not formally made the distinction, has so repeatedly harped on conventions and conventionalists as ideals and idealists that if I were now perversely to call them realities and realists, I should confuse readers of *The Wild Duck* and *Rosmersholm* more than I should help them. Doubtless I shall be reproached for puzzling people by thus limiting the meaning of the term ideal. But what, I ask, is that inevitable passing perplexity compared to the inextricable tangle I must produce if I follow the custom, and use the word indiscriminately in its two violently incompatible senses? If the term realist is objected to on account of some of its modern associations, I can only recommend you, if you must associate it with something else than my own description of its meaning (I do not deal in definitions), to associate it, not with Zola and Maupassant, but with Plato.

Now let us return to our community of 700 Philistines, 299 idealists, and 1 realist. The mere verbal ambiguity against which I have just provided is as nothing beside that which comes of any attempt to express the relations of these three sections, simple as they are, in terms of the ordinary systems of reason and duty. The idealist, higher in the ascent of evolution than the Philistine, yet hates the highest and strikes at him with a dread and rancour of which the easy-going Philistine is guiltless. The man who has risen above the danger and the fear that his acquisitiveness will lead him to theft, his temper to murder, and his affections to debauchery: this is he who is denounced as an arch-scoundrel and libertine, and thus confounded with the lowest because he is the highest. And it is not the ignorant and stupid who maintain this error, but the literate and the cultured. When the true prophet speaks, he is proved to be both rascal and idiot, not by those who have never read of how foolishly such learned demonstrations have come off in the past, but by those who have themselves written volumes on the crucifixions, the burnings, the stonings, the headings and hangings, the Siberia transportations, the calumny and ostracism which have been the lot of the pioneer as well as of the camp follower. It is from men of established literary reputation that we learn that William Blake was mad, that Shelley was spoiled by living in a low set, that Robert Owen was a man who did not know the world, that Ruskin is incapable of comprehending political economy, that Zola is a mere blackguard, and that Ibsen is "a Zola with a wooden leg." The great musician, accepted by the unskilled listener, is vilified by his fellow-musicians: it was the musical culture of Europe that pronounced Wagner the inferior of Mendelssohn and Meyerbeer. The great artist finds his foes among the painters, and not among the men in the street: it is the Royal Academy which places Mr Marcus Stone—not to mention Mr Hodgson—above Mr Burne Jones. It is not rational that it should be so; but it is so, for all that. The realist at last loses patience with ideals altogether, and sees in them only something to blind us, something to numb us, something to murder self in us, something whereby, instead of resisting death, we can disarm it by committing suicide. The idealist, who has taken refuge with the ideals because he hates himself and is ashamed of himself, thinks that all this is so much the better. The realist, who has come to have a deep respect for himself and faith in the validity of his own will, thinks it so much the worse. To the one, human nature, naturally corrupt, is only held back from the excesses of the last years of the Roman empire by self-denying conformity to the ideals. To the other these ideals are only swaddling clothes which man has outgrown, and which insufferably impede his movements. No wonder the two cannot agree. The idealist says, "Realism means egotism, and egotism means depravity." The realist declares that when a man abnegates the will to live and be free in a world of the living and free, seeking only to conform to ideals for the sake of being, not himself, but "a good man," then he is morally dead and rotten, and must be left unheeded to abide his resurrection, if that by good luck arrive before his bodily death. Unfortunately, this is the sort of speech that nobody but a realist understands. It will be more amusing as well as more convincing to take an actual example of an idealist criticising a realist.

III.
THE WOMANLY WOMAN.

EVERYBODY remembers the "Diary of Marie Bashkirtseff." An outline of it, with a running commentary, was given in the *Review of Reviews* (June 1890) by the editor, Mr William Stead, a sort of modern Julian the Apostate, who, having gained an immense following by a public service in rendering which he had to perform a realistic feat of a somewhat scandalous character, entered upon a campaign with the object of establishing the ideal of sexual "purity" as a condition of public life. As he retains his best qualities—faith in himself, wilfulness, conscientious unscrupulousness — he can always make himself heard. Prominent among his ideals is an ideal of womanliness. In support of that ideal he will, like all idealists, make and believe any statement, however obviously and grotesquely unreal. When he found Marie Bashkirtseff's account of herself utterly incompatible with the account of a woman's mind given to him by his ideal, he was confronted with the dilemma that either Marie was not a woman or else his ideal did not correspond to nature. He actually accepted the former alternative. "Of the distinctively womanly," he says, "there is in her but little trace. She was the very antithesis of a true woman." Mr Stead's next difficulty was, that self-control, being a leading quality in his ideal, could not have been possessed by Marie: otherwise she would have been more like his ideal. Nevertheless he had to record that she, without any compulsion from circumstances, made herself a highly skilled artist by working ten hours a day for six years. Let anyone who thinks that this is no evidence of self-control just try it for six months. Mr Stead's verdict nevertheless, was "No self-control." However, his fundamental quarrel with Marie came out in the following lines. "Marie," he said, "was artist, musician, wit, philosopher, student, anything you like but a natural woman with a heart to love, and a soul to find its supreme satisfaction in sacrifice for lover or for child." Now of all the idealist abominations that make society pestiferous, I doubt if there be any so mean as that of forcing self-sacrifice on a woman under pretence that she likes it; and, if she ventures to contradict the pretence, declaring her no true woman. In India they carried this piece of idealism to the length of declaring that a wife could not bear to survive her husband, but would be prompted by her own faithful, loving, beautiful nature to offer up her life on the pyre which consumed his dead body. The astonishing thing is that women, sooner than be branded as unsexed wretches, allowed themselves to be stupefied with drink, and in that unwomanly condition burnt alive. British Philistinism put down widow idealizing with the strong hand; and suttee is abolished in India. The English form of it still survives; and Mr Stead, the rescuer of the children, is one of its high-priests. Imagine his feelings on coming across this entry in a woman's diary, "I love myself." Or this, "I swear solemnly —by the Gospels, by the passion of Christ, by MYSELF—that in four years I will be famous." The young woman was positively proposing to exercise for her own sake all the powers that were given her, in Mr Stead's opinion, solely that she might sacrifice them for her lover or child! No wonder he is driven to exclaim again, "She was very clever, no doubt; but woman she was not." Now observe this notable result. Marie Bashkirtseff, instead of being a less agreeable person than the ordinary female conformer to the ideal of womanliness, was conspicuously the reverse. Mr Stead himself wrote as one infatuated with her mere diary, and pleased himself by representing her as a person who fascinated everybody, and was a source of delight to all about her by the mere exhilaration and hope-giving atmosphere of her wilfulness. The truth is, that in real life a self-sacrificing woman, or, as Mr Stead would put it, a womanly woman, is not only taken advantage of, but disliked as well for her pains. No *man* pretends that his soul finds its supreme satisfaction in self sacrifice: such an affectation would stamp him as a coward and weakling: the manly man is he who takes the Bashkirtseff view of himself. But men are not the less loved on this account. No one ever feels helpless by the side of the self-helper; whilst the self-sacrificer is always a drag, a responsibility, a reproach, an everlasting and unnatural trouble with whom no really strong soul can live. Only those who have helped themselves know how to help others, and to respect their right to help themselves.

Although romantic idealists generally insist on self-surrender as an indispensable element in true womanly love, its repulsive effect is well-known and feared in practice by both sexes. The extreme instance is the reckless self-abandonment seen in the infatuation of passionate sexual desire. Everyone who becomes the object of that infatuation shrinks from it instinctively. Love loses its charm when it is not free; and whether the compulsion is that of custom and law, or of infatuation, the effect is the same: it becomes valueless. The desire to give inspires no affection unless there is also the power to withhold; and the successful wooer, in both sexes alike, is the one who can stand out for honourable conditions, and, failing them, go without. Such conditions are evidently not offered to either sex by the legal marriage of to-day; for it is the intense repugnance inspired by the compulsory character of the legalized conjugal relation that leads, first to the idealization of marriage whilst it remains indispensable as a means of perpetuating society; then to its modification by divorce and by the abolition of penalties for refusal to comply with judicial orders for restitution of conjugal rights; and finally to its disuse and disappearance as the responsibility for the maintenance and education of the rising generation is shifted from the parent to the community.*

---

* A dissertation on the anomalies and impossibilities of the marriage law at its present stage would be too far out of the main course of my argument to be introduced in the text above; but it may be well to point out in passing to those who regard marriage as an inviolable and inviolate institution, that necessity has already forced us to tamper with it to such an extent that at this moment the highest court in the kingdom is face to face with a husband and wife, the one demanding whether a woman may saddle him with all the responsibilities of a

Although the growing repugnance to face the Church of England marriage service has led many celebrants to omit those passages which frankly explain the object of the institution, we are not likely to dispense with legal ties and obligations, and trust wholly to the permanence of love, until the continuity of society no longer depends on the private nursery. Love, as a practical factor in society, is still a mere appetite. That higher development of it which Ibsen shews us occurring in the case of Rebecca West in *Rosmersholm* is only known to most of us by the descriptions of great poets, who themselves, as their biographies prove, have often known it, not by sustained experience, but only by brief glimpses. And it is never a first-fruit of their

---

husband and then refuse to live with him, and the other asking whether the law allows her husband to commit abduction, imprisonment and rape upon her. If the court says Yes to the husband, marriage is made intolerable for men; if it says Yes to the wife, marriage is made intolerable for women; and as this exhausts the possible alternatives, it is clear that provision must be made for the dissolution of such marriages if the institution is to be maintained at all, which it must be until its social function is otherwise provided for. Marriage is thus, by force of circumstances, compelled to buy extension of life by extension of divorce, much as if a fugitive should try to delay a pursuing wolf by throwing portions of his own heart to it.

The Womanly Woman. 37

love affairs. Tannhäuser may die in the conviction that one moment of the emotion he felt with St Elizabeth was fuller and happier than all the hours of passion he spent with Venus; but that does not alter the fact that love began for him with Venus, and that its earlier tentatives towards the final goal were attended with relapses. Now Tannhauser's passion for Venus is a development of the humdrum fondness of the bourgeois Jack for his Gill, a development at once higher and more dangerous, just as idealism is at once higher and more dangerous than Philistinism. The fondness is the germ of the passion: the passion is the germ of the more perfect love. When Blake told men that through excess they would learn moderation, he knew that the way for the present lay through the Venusberg, and that the race would assuredly not perish there as some individuals have, and as the Puritan fears we all shall unless we find a way round. Also he no doubt foresaw the time when our children would be born on the other side of it, and so be spared that fiery purgation.

But the very facts that Blake is still commonly regarded as a crazy visionary, and that the current criticism of *Rosmersholm* entirely fails even to notice the evolution of Rebecca's passion for Rosmer into her love for him, much more to credit the moral transfiguration which accompanies it, shew how absurd it would be to pretend, for the sake of edification, that the ordinary marriage of to-day is a union between a William Blake and a Rebecca West, or that it would be possible, even if it were enlightened policy, to deny the satisfaction of the sexual appetite to persons who have not reached that stage. An overwhelming majority of such marriages as are not purely *de convenance*, are entered into for the gratification of that appetite either in its crudest form or veiled only by those idealistic illusions which the youthful imagination weaves so wonderfully under the stimulus of desire, and which older people indulgently laugh at. This being so, it is not surprising that our society, being directly dominated by men, comes to regard Woman, not as an end in herself like Man, but solely as a means of ministering to his appetite. The ideal wife is one who does everything that the ideal husband likes, and nothing else. Now to treat a person as a means instead of an end is to deny that person's right to live. And to be treated as a means to such an end as sexual intercourse with those who deny one's right to live is insufferable to any human being. Woman, if she dares face the fact that she is being so treated, must either loathe herself or else rebel. As a rule, when circumstances enable her to rebel successfully—

for instance, when the accident of genius enables her to "lose her character" without losing her employment or cutting herself off from the society she values—she does rebel; but circumstances seldom do. Does she then loathe herself? By no means: she deceives herself in the idealist fashion by denying that the love which her suitor offers her is tainted with sexual appetite at all. It is, she declares, a beautiful, disinterested, pure, sublime devotion to another by which a man's life is exalted and purified, and a woman's rendered blest. And of all the cynics, the filthiest to her mind is the one who sees, in the man making honourable proposals to his future wife, nothing but the human male seeking his female. The man himself keeps her confirmed in her illusion; for the truth is unbearable to him too: he wants to form an affectionate tie, and not to drive a degrading bargain. After all, the germ of the highest love is in them both, though as yet it is no more than the appetite they are disguising so carefully from themselves. Consequently every stockbroker who has just brought his business up to marrying point woos in terms of the romantic illusion; and it is agreed between the two that their marriage shall realize the romantic ideal. Then comes the breakdown of the plan. The young wife finds that her husband is neglecting her for his business; that his interests, his activities, his whole life except that one part of it to which only a cynic ever referred before her marriage, lies away from home, and that her business is to sit there and mope until she is wanted. Then what can she do? If she complains, he, the self-helper, can do without her; whilst she is dependent on him for her position, her livelihood, her place in society, her home, her name, her very bread. All this is brought home to her by the first burst of displeasure her complaints provoke. Fortunately, things do not remain for ever at this point—perhaps the most wretched in a woman's life. The self-respect she has lost as a wife she regains as a mother, in which capacity her use and importance to the community compare favourably with those of most men of business. She is wanted in the house, wanted in the market, wanted by the children; and now, instead of weeping because her husband is away in the city, thinking of stocks and shares instead of his ideal woman, she would regard his presence in the house all day as an intolerable nuisance. And so, though she is completely disillusioned on the subject of ideal love, yet, since it has not turned out so badly after all, she countenances the illusion still from the point of view that it is a useful and harmless means of getting boys and girls to marry and settle down. And this conviction is the stronger in her because she feels that if she had known as much about marriage the day before her wedding as she did six months after, it would have been extremely hard to induce her to get married at all.

This prosaic solution is satisfactory only within certain limits. It depends altogether upon the accident of the woman having some natural vocation for domestic management and the care of children, as well as on the husband being fairly good-natured and livable-with. Hence arises the idealist illusion that a vocation for domestic management and the care of children is natural to women, and that women who lack them are not women at all, but members of the third, or Bashkirtseff sex. Even if this were true, it is obvious that if the Bashkirtseffs are to be allowed to live, they have a right to suitable institutions just as much as men and women. But it is not true. The domestic career is no more natural to all women than the military career is natural to all men; although it may be necessary that every able-bodied woman should be called on to risk her life in childbed just as it may be necessary that every man should be called on to risk his life in the battlefield. It is of course quite true that the majority of women are kind to children and prefer their own to other people's. But exactly the same thing is true of the majority of men, who nevertheless do not consider that their proper sphere is the nursery. The case may be illustrated more grotesquely by the fact that the majority of women who have dogs, are kind to them, and prefer their own dogs to other people's; yet it is not proposed that women should restrict their activities to the rearing of puppies. If we have come to think that the nursery and the kitchen are the natural sphere of a woman, we have done so exactly as English children come to think that a cage is the natural sphere of a parrot—because they have never seen one anywhere else. No doubt there are Philistine parrots who agree with their owners that it is better to be in a cage than out, so long as there is plenty of hempseed and Indian corn there. There may even be idealist parrots who persuade themselves that the mission of a parrot is to minister to the happiness of a private family by whistling and saying "Pretty Polly," and that it is in the sacrifice of its liberty to this altruistic pursuit that a true parrot finds the supreme satisfaction of its soul. I will not go so far as to affirm that there are theological parrots who are convinced that imprisonment is the will of God because it is unpleasant; but I am confident that there are rationalist parrots who can demonstrate that it would be a cruel kindness to let a parrot out to fall a prey to cats, or at least to forget its accomplishments and coarsen its naturally delicate fibres in an unprotected struggle for existence. Still, the only parrot a free-souled person can sympathize with is the one that insists on being let out as the first condition of its making itself agreeable. A selfish bird, you may say : one that puts its own gratification before that of the family which is so fond of it —before even the greatest happiness of the greatest number: one that, in aping the independent spirit of a man, has unparroted itself and become a creature that has neither the home-loving nature of a bird nor the strength and enterprise of a mastiff. All the same, you respect that parrot in spite of your conclusive reasoning ; and if it persists, you will have either to let it out or kill it.

The sum of the matter is that unless Woman repudiates her womanliness, her duty to her husband, to her children, to society, to the law, and to everyone but herself, she cannot emancipate herself. But her duty to herself is no duty at all, since a debt is cancelled when the debtor and creditor are the same person. Its payment is simply a fulfilment of the individual will, upon which all duty is a restriction, founded on the conception of the will as naturally malign and devilish. Therefore Woman has to repudiate duty altogether. In that repudiation lies her freedom; for it is false to say that Woman is now directly the slave of Man: she is the immediate slave of duty; and as man's path to freedom is strewn with the wreckage of the duties and ideals he has trampled on, so must hers be. She may indeed mask her iconoclasm by proving in rationalist fashion, as Man has often done for the sake of a quiet life, that all these discarded idealist conceptions will be fortified instead of shattered by her emancipation. To a person with a turn for logic, such proofs are as easy as playing the piano is to Paderewski. But it will not be true. A whole basketful of ideals of the most sacred quality will be smashed by the achievement of equality for women and men. Those who shrink from such a clatter and breakage may comfort themselves with the reflection that the replacement of the broken goods will be prompt and certain. It is always a case of "The ideal is dead: long live the ideal!" And the advantage of the work of destruction is, that every new ideal is less of an illusion than the one it has supplanted; so that the destroyer of ideals, though denounced as an enemy of society, is in fact sweeping the world clear of lies.

My digression is now over. Having traversed

my loop as I promised, and come back to Man's repudiation of duty by way of Woman's, I may at last proceed to give some more particular account of Ibsen's work without further preoccupation with Mr Clement Scott's protest, or the many others of which it is the type. For we now see that the pioneer must necessarily provoke such outcry as he repudiates duties, tramples on ideals, profanes what was sacred, sanctifies what was infamous, always driving his plough through gardens of pretty weeds in spite of the laws made against trespassers for the protection of the worms which feed on the roots, letting in light and air to hasten the putrefaction of decaying matter, and everywhere proclaiming that "the old beauty is no longer beautiful, the new truth no longer true." He can do no less; and what more and what else he does it is not given to all of his generation to understand. And if any man does not understand, and cannot foresee the harvest, what can he do but cry out in all sincerity against such destruction, until at last we come to know the cry of the blind like any other street cry, and to bear with it as an honest cry, albeit a false alarm.

IV.

THE PLAYS

BRAND.

WE are now prepared to learn without misgiving that a typical Ibsen play is one in which the "leading lady" is an unwomanly woman, and the "villain" an idealist. It follows that the leading lady is not a heroine of the Drury Lane type; nor does the villain forge or assassinate, since he is a villain by virtue of his determination to do nothing wrong. Therefore readers of Ibsen—not playgoers—have sometimes so far misconceived him as to suppose that his villains are examples rather than warnings, and that the mischief and ruin which attend their actions are but the tribulations from which the soul comes out purified as gold from the furnace. In fact, the beginning of Ibsen's European reputation was the edification with which the pious of Scandinavia received his great dramatic poem *Brand*. Brand the priest is an idealist of heroic earnestness, strength, and courage. He declares himself the champion, not of things as they are, nor of things as they can be made, but of things as they ought to be. Things as they ought to be mean for him things as ordered by men conformed to his ideal of the perfect Adam, who, again, is not man as he is or can be, but man conformed to all the ideals—man as it is his duty to be. In insisting on this conformity, Brand spares neither himself nor anyone else. Life is nothing: self is nothing: the perfect Adam is everything. The imperfect Adam does not fall in with these views. A peasant whom he urges to cross a glacier in a fog because it is his duty to visit his dying daughter, not only flatly declines, but endeavours forcibly to prevent Brand from risking his own life. Brand knocks him down, and sermonizes him with fierce earnestness and scorn. Presently Brand has to cross a fiord in a storm to reach a dying man who, having committed a series of murders, wants "consolation" from a priest. Brand cannot go alone: someone must hold the rudder of his boat whilst he manages the sail. The fisher folk, in whom the old Adam is strong, do not adopt his estimate of the gravity of the situation, and refuse to go. A woman, fascinated by his heroism and idealism, goes. That ends in their marriage, and in the birth of a child to which they become deeply attached. Then Brand aspiring from height to height of devotion to his ideal, plunges from depth to depth of murderous cruelty. First the child must die from the severity of the climate because Brand must not flinch from the post of duty and leave his congregation exposed to the peril of getting an inferior preacher in his place. Then he forces his wife to give the clothes of the dead child to a gipsy whose baby needs them. The bereaved mother does not grudge the gift; but she wants to hold back only one little garment as a relic of her darling. But Brand sees in this reservation the imperfection of the imperfect Eve. He forces her to regard the situation as a choice between the relic and his ideal. She sacrifices the relic to the ideal, and then dies, broken-hearted. Having killed her, and thereby placed himself beyond ever daring to doubt the idealism upon whose altar he has immolated her —having also refused to go to his mother's deathbed because she compromises with his principles in disposing of her property, he is hailed by the people as a saint, and finds his newly built church too small for his congregation. So he calls upon them to follow him to worship God in His own temple, the mountains. After a brief practical experience of this arrangement, they change their minds, and stone him. The very mountains themselves stone him, indeed; for he is killed by an avalanche.

PEER GYNT.

Brand dies a saint, having caused more intense suffering by his saintliness than the most talented sinner could possibly have done with twice his opportunities. Ibsen does not leave this to be inferred. In another dramatic poem he gives us an accomplished rascal named Peer Gynt, an idealist who avoids Brand's errors by setting up as his ideal the realization of himself by the utter satisfaction of his own will. In this he would seem to be on the path to which Ibsen himself points; and indeed all who know the two plays will agree that whether or no it was better to be Peer Gynt than Brand, it was beyond all question better to be the mother or the sweetheart of Peer, scapegrace and liar as he was, than mother or wife to the saintly Brand. Brand would force his ideal on all men and women: Peer Gynt keeps his ideal for himself alone. it is indeed implicit in the ideal itself that it should be unique—that he alone should have the force to realize it. For Peer's first boyish notion of the self-realized man is not the saint, but the demigod whose indomitable will is stronger than destiny, the fighter, the master, the man whom no woman can resist, the mighty hunter, the knight of a thousand adventures,—the model, in short, of the lover in a lady's novel, or the hero in a boy's romance. Now, no such person exists, or ever did exist, or ever can exist. The man who cultivates an indomitable will and refuses to make way for anything or anybody, soon finds that he cannot hold a street crossing against a tram car, much less a world against the whole human race. Only by plunging into illusions to which every fact gives the lie can he persuade himself that his will is a force that can overcome all other forces, or that it is less conditioned by circumstances than is a wheelbarrow. However, Peer Gynt, being imaginative enough to conceive his ideal, is also imaginative enough to find illusions to hide its unreality, and to persuade himself that Peer Gynt, the shabby countryside loafer, is Peer Gynt, Emperor of Himself, as he writes over the door of his hut in the mountains. His hunting feats are invented ; his military genius has no solider foundation than a street fight with a smith; and his reputation as an adventurous daredevil he has to gain by the bravado of carrying off the bride from a wedding at which the guests snub him. Only in the mountains can he enjoy his illusions undisturbed by ridicule · yet even in the mountains he finds obstacles which he cannot force his way through, obstacles which withstand him as spirits with voices, telling him that he must go round. But he will not : he will go forward : he will cut his path sword in hand, in spite of fate. All the same, he has to go round ; for the world-will is without Peer Gynt as well as within him. Then he tries the supernatural, only to find that it means nothing more than the transmogrifying of squalid realities by lies and pretences. Still, like our amateurs of thaumaturgy, he is willing to enter into a conspiracy of make-believe up to a certain point When the Trold king's daughter appears as a repulsive ragged creature riding on a pig, he is ready to accept her as a beautiful princess on a noble steed, on condition that she accepts his mother's tumble-down farmhouse, with the broken window panes stopped up with old clouts, as a splendid castle. He will go with her among the Trolds, and pretend that the gruesome ravine in which they hold their orgies is a glorious palace, he will partake of their filthy food and declare it nectar and ambrosia ; he will applaud their obscene antics as exquisite dancing, and their discordant din as divine music ; but when they finally propose to slit his eyes so that he may see and hear these things, not as they are, but as he has been pretending to see and hear them, he draws back, resolved to be himself even in self-deception. He leaves the mountains and becomes a prosperous man of business in America, highly respectable and ready for any profitable speculation—slave trade, Bible trade, whisky trade, missionary trade, anything! In this phase he takes to piety, and persuades himself, like Mr Stanley, that he is under the special care of God. This opinion is shaken by an adventure in which he is marooned on the African coast; and it is not restored until the treacherous friends who marooned him are destroyed before his eyes by the blowing-up of the steam yacht they have just stolen from him, when he utters his celebrated exclamation, " Ah, God is a Father to me after all , but economical he certainly is not." He finds a white horse in the desert, and is accepted on its account as the Messiah by an Arab tribe, a success which moves him to declare that now at last he is really worshipped for himself, whereas in America people only respected his breast-pin, the symbol of his money. In commerce, too, he reflects, his eminence was a mere matter of chance, whilst as a prophet he is eminent by pure natural fitness for the post. This is ended by his falling in love with a dancing-girl, who, after leading him into every sort of undignified and ludicrous extravagance, ranging from his hailing her as the Eternal-Feminine of Goethe to the more practical folly of giving her his white horse and all his prophetic finery, runs away with the spoil, and leaves him once more helpless and alone in the desert. He wanders until he comes to the great Sphinx, beside which he finds a German gentleman in great perplexity as to who the Sphinx is. Peer Gynt, seeing in that impassive, immovable, majestic figure, a symbol of his own ideal, is able to tell the German gentleman at once that the Sphinx is itself. This explanation dazzles the German, who, after some further discussion of the philosophy of self-realization, invites Peer Gynt to accompany him to a club of learned men in Cairo, who are ripe for enlightenment on this very question. Peer, delighted, accompanies the German to the club, which turns out to be a madhouse in which the lunatics have broken loose and locked up their keepers. It is in this madhouse, and by these madmen, that Peer Gynt is at last crowned Emperor of Himself. He receives their homage as he lies in the dust fainting with terror.

As an old man, Peer Gynt, returning to the scenes of his early adventures, is troubled with the prospect of meeting a certain button moulder who threatens to make short work of his realized self by melting it down into buttons in his crucible with a heap of other button-material. Immediately the old exaltation of the self-realizer is changed into an unspeakable dread of the button-moulder Death, to avoid whom Peer Gynt will commit any act, even to pushing a drowning man from the spar he is clinging to in a shipwreck lest it should not suffice to support two. At last he finds a deserted sweetheart of his youth still waiting for him and still believing in him. In the imagination of this old woman he finds the ideal Peer Gynt; whilst in himself, the loafer, the braggart, the confederate of sham magicians, the Charleston speculator, the false prophet, the dancing-girl's dupe, the bedlam emperor, the selfish thruster of the drowning man into the waves, there is nothing heroic—nothing but commonplace self-seeking and shirking, cowardice and sensuality, veiled only by the romantic fancies of the born liar. With this crowningly unreal realization he is left to face the button-moulder as best he can.

Peer Gynt has puzzled a good many people by Ibsen's fantastic and subtle treatment of its thesis. It is so far a difficult play, that the ideal of unconditional self-realization, however familiar its suggestions may be to the ambitious reader, is not at all understood by him, much less formulated as a proposition in metaphysics. When it is stated to him by some one who does understand it, he unhesitatingly dismisses it as idiotic; and it is because he is perfectly right in doing so—because it is idiotic in the most accurate sense of the term—that he finds such difficulty in recognizing it as the common ideal of his own prototype, the pushing, competitive, success-loving man who is the hero of the modern world.

There is nothing novel in Ibsen's dramatic method of reducing these ideals to absurdity. Exactly as Cervantes took the old ideal of chivalry, and shewed what came of a man attempting to act as if it were real, so Ibsen takes the ideals of Brand and Peer Gynt, and treats them in the very same manner. Don Quixote acts as if he were a perfect knight in a world of giants and distressed damsels instead of a country gentleman in a land of innkeepers and farm wenches; Brand acts as if he were the perfect Adam in a world where, by resolute rejection of all compromise with imperfection, it was immediately possible to change the rainbow "bridge between flesh and spirit" into as enduring a structure as the tower of Babel was intended to be, thereby restoring man to the condition in which he walked with God in the garden; and Peer Gynt tries to act as if he had in him a special force that could be concentrated so as to prevail over all other forces. They ignore the real—ignore what they are and where they are, not only, like Nelson, shutting their eyes to the signals that a brave man may disregard, but insanely steering straight on the rocks that no resolution can prevail against. Observe that neither Cervantes nor Ibsen is incredulous, in the

Philistine way, as to the power of ideals over men. Don Quixote, Brand, and Peer Gynt are, all three, men of action seeking to realize their ideals in deeds. However ridiculous Don Quixote makes himself, you cannot dislike or despise him, much less think that it would have been better for him to have been a Philistine like Sancho; and Peer Gynt, selfish rascal as he is, is not unlovable. Brand, made terrible by the consequences of his idealism to others, is heroic. Their castles in the air are more beautiful than castles of brick and mortar, but one cannot live in them; and they seduce men into pretending that every hovel is such a castle, just as Peer Gynt pretended that the Trold king's den was a palace.

EMPEROR AND GALILEAN.

When Ibsen, by merely giving the rein to the creative impulse of his poetic nature, had produced *Brand* and *Peer Gynt*, he was nearly forty. His will, in setting his imagination to work, had produced a great puzzle for his intellect. In no case does the difference between the will and the intellect come out more clearly than in that of the poet, save only that of the lover. Had Ibsen died in 1867, he, like many another great poet, would have gone to his grave without having ever rationally understood his own meaning.

Nay, if in that year an intellectual expert—a commentator, as we call him—had gone to Ibsen and offered him the explanation of *Brand* which he himself must have arrived at before he constructed *Ghosts* and *The Wild Duck*, he would perhaps have repudiated it with as much disgust as a maiden would feel if anyone were brutal enough to give her the physiological *rationale* of her dreams of meeting a fairy prince. It is only the naif who goes to the creative artist with absolute confidence in receiving an answer to his " What does this passage mean?" That is the very question which the poet's own intellect, which had no part in the conception of the poem, may be asking him. And this curiosity of the intellect—this restless life in it which differentiates it from dead machinery, and which troubles our lesser artists but little, is one of the marks of the greater sort Shakespear, in *Hamlet*, made a drama of the self-questioning that came upon him when his intellect rose up in alarm, as well it might, against the vulgar optimism of his *Henry V.*, and yet could mend it to no better purpose than by the equally vulgar pessimism of *Troilus and Cressida*. Dante took pains to understand himself: so did Goethe. Richard Wagner, one of the greatest poets of our own day, has left us as many volumes of criticism of art and life as he has left musical scores; and he has expressly described how the intellectual activity which he brought to the analysis of his music dramas was in abeyance during their creation. Just so do we find Ibsen, after composing his two great dramatic poems, entering on a struggle to become intellectually conscious of what he had done.

We have seen that with Shakespear such an effort became itself creative and produced a drama of questioning. With Ibsen the same thing occurred: he harked back to an abandoned project of his, and wrote two huge dramas on the subject of the apostasy of the Emperor Julian. In this work we find him at first preoccupied with a piece of old-fashioned freethinking—the dilemma that moral responsibility presupposes free-will, and that free-will sets man above God. Cain, who slew because he willed, willed because he must, and must have willed to slay because he was himself, comes upon the stage to claim that murder is fertile, and death the ground of life, though he cannot say what is the ground of death. Judas, who betrayed under the same necessity, wants to know whether, since the Master chose him, he chose him foreknowingly. This part of the drama has no very deep significance. It is easy to invent conundrums which dogmatic evangelicalism cannot answer; and no doubt, whilst it was still a nine days' wonder that evangelicalism could not solve all enigmas, such invention seemed something much deeper than the mere intellectual chess-play which it is seen to be now that the nine days are past. In his occasional weakness for such conundrums, and later on in his harping on the hereditary transmission of disease, we see Ibsen's active intellect busy, not only with the problems peculiar to his own plays, but with the fatalism and pessimism of the middle of our century, when the typical advanced culture was attainable by reading Strauss's *Leben Jesu*, the popularizations of Helmholtz and Darwin by Tyndall and Huxley, and George Eliot's novels, vainly protested against by Ruskin as peopled with "the sweepings of a Pentonville omnibus." The traces of this period in Ibsen's writings show how well he knew the crushing weight with which the sordid cares of the ordinary struggle for money and respectability fell on the world when the romance of the creeds was discredited, and progress seemed for the moment to mean, not the growth of the spirit of man, but an effect of the survival of the fittest brought about by the destruction of the unfit, all the most frightful examples of this systematic destruction being thrust into the utmost prominence by those who were fighting the Church with Mill's favourite dialectical weapon, the incompatibility of divine omnipotence with divine benevolence. His plays are full of evidence of his overwhelming sense of the necessity for rousing the individual into self-assertion against this numbing fatalism; and yet he never seems to have freed his intellect wholly from an acceptance of its scientific validity. That it only accounted for progress at all on the hypothesis of a continuous increase in the severity of the conditions of existence,—that is, on an assumption of just the reverse of what was actually taking place—appears to have escaped Ibsen as completely as it has escaped Professor Huxley himself. It is true that he did not allow himself to be stopped by this gloomy fortress of pessimism and materialism: his genius pushed him past it, but without intellectually reducing it; and the result is, that as far as one can guess, he believes to this day that it is impregnable, not dreaming that it has been demolished, and that too with ridiculous ease, by the mere march behind him of the working class, which, by its freedom from the characteristic bias of the middle classes, has escaped their characteristic illusions, and solved many of the enigmas which they found insoluble because they wished to find them so. His prophetic belief in the spontaneous growth of the will makes him a meliorist without reference to the operation of natural selection; but his impression of the light thrown by physical and biological science on the facts of life seems to be the gloomy one of the period at which he must have received his education in these departments. External nature often plays her most ruthless and destructive part in his works, which have an extraordinary fascination for the pessimists of that school, in spite of the incompatibility of his individualism with that mechanical utilitarian ethic of theirs which treats Man as the sport of every circumstance, and ignores his will altogether

Another inessential but very prominent feature in Ibsen's dramas will be understood easily by anyone who has observed how a change of religious faith intensifies our concern about our own salvation. An ideal, pious or secular, is practically used as a standard of conduct; and whilst it remains unquestioned, the simple rule of right is to conform to it In the theological stage, when the Bible is accepted as the revelation of God's will, the pious man, when in doubt as to whether he is acting rightly or wrongly, quiets his misgivings by searching the Scripture until he finds a text which endorses his action.* The rationalist, for whom the Bible

---

* As such misgivings seldom arise except when the conscience revolts against the contemplated action, an appeal to Scripture to justify a point of conduct is generally found in practice to be an attempt to excuse a crime.

has no authority, brings his conduct to such tests as asking himself, after Kant, how it would be if everyone did as he proposes to do; or by calculating the effect of his action on the greatest happiness of the greatest number; or by judging whether the liberty of action he is claiming infringes the equal liberty of others, &c. &c. Most men are ingenious enough to pass examinations of this kind successfully in respect to everything they really want to do. But in periods of transition, as, for instance, when faith in the infallibility of the Bible is shattered, and faith in that of reason not yet perfected, men's uncertainty as to the rightness and wrongness of their actions keeps them in a continual perplexity, amid which casuistry seems the most important branch of intellectual activity. Life, as depicted by Ibsen, is very full of it. We find the great double drama of *Emperor and Galilean* occupied at first with Julian's case regarded as a case of conscience It is compared, in the manner already described, with the cases of Cain and Judas, the three men being introduced as "corner stones under the wrath of necessity," "great freedmen under necessity," and so forth. The qualms of Julian are theatrically effective in producing the most exciting suspense as to whether he will dare to choose between Christ and the imperial purple;

but the mere exhibition of a man struggling between his ambition and his creed belongs to a phase of intellectual interest which Ibsen had passed even before the production of *Brand*, when he wrote his *Kongs Emnerne* or *The Pretenders*. *Emperor and Galilean* might have been appropriately, if prosaically, named *The Mistake of Maximus the Mystic*. It is Maximus who forces the choice on Julian, not as between ambition and principle—between Paganism and Christianity—between "the old beauty that is no longer beautiful and the new truth that is no longer true," but between Christ and Julian himself. Maximus knows that there is no going back to "the first empire" of pagan sensualism. "The second empire," Christian or self-abnegatory idealism, is already rotten at heart. "The third empire" is what he looks for—the empire of Man asserting the eternal validity of his own will. He who can see that not on Olympus, not nailed to the cross, but in himself is God; he is the man to build Brand's bridge between the flesh and the spirit, establishing this third empire in which the spirit shall not be unknown, nor the flesh starved, nor the will tortured and baffled Thus throughout the first part of the double drama we have Julian prompted step by step to the stupendous conviction that he and not the Galilean is God. His final resolution to seize the throne is expressed in his interruption of the Lord's prayer, which he hears intoned by worshippers in church as he wrestles in the gloom of the catacombs with his own fears and the entreaties and threats of his soldiers urging him to take the final decisive step. At the cue "Lead us not into temptation; but deliver us from evil" he rushes to the church with his soldiers, exclaiming "For mine is the kingdom." Yet he halts on the threshold, dazzled by the light, as his follower Sallust points the declaration by adding,—" and the kingdom, and the power, and the glory."

Once on the throne Julian becomes a mere pedant-tyrant, trying to revive Paganism mechanically by cruel enforcement of external conformity to its rites. In his moments of exaltation he half grasps the meaning of Maximus, only to relapse presently and pervert it into a grotesque mixture of superstition and monstrous vanity. We have him making such speeches as this, worthy of Peer Gynt at his most ludicrous. "Has not Plato long ago enunciated the truth that only a god can rule over men? What did he mean by that saying? Answer me: what did he mean? Far be it from me to assert that Plato—incomparable sage though he was—had any individual, even the greatest, in his prophetic eye," &c. In this frame of mind Christ appears to him, not as the prototype of himself, as Maximus would have him feel, but as a rival god over whom he must prevail at all costs. It galls him to think that the Galilean still reigns in the hearts of men whilst the emperor can only extort lip honour from them by brute force; for in his wildest excesses of egotism he never so loses his saving sense of the realities of things as to mistake the trophies of persecution for the fruits of faith. "Tell me who shall conquer," he demands of Maximus, "— the emperor or the Galilean?"

"Both the emperor and the Galilean shall succumb," says Maximus. "Whether in our time or in hundreds of years I know not; but so it shall be when the right man comes."

"Who is the right man?" says Julian.

"He who shall swallow up both emperor and Galilean," replies the seer. "Both shall succumb; but you shall not therefore perish. Does not the child succumb in the youth and the youth in the man: yet neither child nor youth perishes. You know I have never approved of your policy as emperor. You have tried to make the youth a child again The empire of the flesh is fallen a prey to the empire of the spirit. But the empire of the spirit is not final, any more than the youth is. You have tried to hinder the youth from growing—from becoming a man. Oh fool, who have drawn your sword against that which is to be—against the third empire, in which the twin-natured shall reign. For him the Jews have a name. They call him Messiah, and are waiting for him."

Still Julian stumbles on the threshold of the idea without entering into it He is galled out of all comprehension by the rivalry of the Galilean, and asks despairingly who shall break his power. Then Maximus drives the lesson home.

MAXIMUS.—Is it not written, "Thou shalt have none other gods but me"?

JULIAN.—Yes—yes—yes.

MAXIMUS.—The seer of Nazareth did not preach this god or that: he said "God is I. I am God."

JULIAN.—And that is what makes the emperor powerless. The third empire? The Messiah? Not the Jews' Messiah, but the Messiah of the two empires, the spirit and the world—?

MAXIMUS.—The God-Emperor.

JULIAN.—The Emperor-God.

MAXIMUS.—Logos in Pan, Pan in Logos.

JULIAN.—How is he begotten?

MAXIMUS.—He is self-begotten in the man who wills.

But it is of no use. Maximus's idea is a synthesis of relations in which not only is Christ God in exactly the same sense as that in which Julian is God, but Julian is Christ as well. The persistence of Julian's jealousy of the Galilean shews that he has not comprehended the synthesis at all, but only seized on that part of it which flatters his own egotism. And since this part is only valid as a constituent of the synthesis, and has no reality when isolated from it, it cannot by itself convince Julian. In vain does Maximus repeat his lesson in every sort of parable, and in such pregnant questions as " How do you know, Julian, that you were not in him whom you now persecute?" He can only wreak him to utter commands to the winds, and to exclaim, in the excitement of burning his fleet on the borders of Persia, " The third empire is here, Maximus. I feel that the Messiah of the earth lives within me. The spirit has become flesh and the flesh spirit. All creation lies within my will and power. More than the fleet is burning. In that glowing, swirling pyre the crucified Galilean is burning to ashes; and the earthly emperor is burning with the Galilean. But from the ashes shall arise, phœnix-like, the God of earth and the Emperor of the spirit in one, in one, in one." At which point he is informed that the Persian refugee whose information has emboldened him to burn his ships, has fled from the camp and is a manifest spy. From that moment he is a broken man. In his next and last emergency, when the Persians fall upon his camp, his first desperate exclamation is a vow to sacrifice to the gods "To what gods, oh fool?" cries Maximus. "Where are they; and what are they?" "I will sacrifice to this god and that god—I will sacrifice to many," he answers desperately. "One or other must surely hear me *I must call on something without me and above me.*" A flash of lightning seems to him a response from above; and with this encouragement he throws himself into the fight, clinging, like Macbeth, to an ambiguous oracle which leads him to suppose that only in the Phrygian regions need he fear defeat. He imagines he sees the Nazarene in the ranks of the enemy; and in fighting madly to reach him he is struck down, in the name of Christ, by one of his own soldiers. Then his one Christian general, Jovian, calls on his "believing brethren" to give Cæsar what is Cæsar's. Declaring that the heavens are open and the angels coming to the rescue with their swords of fire, he rallies the Galileans of whom Julian has made slave-soldiers. The pagan free legions, crying out that the god of the Galileans is on the Roman side, and that he is the strongest, follow Jovian as he charges the enemy, who fly in all directions whilst Julian, sinking back from a vain effort to rise, exclaims, "Thou hast conquered, oh Galilean."

Julian dies quietly in his tent, averring, in reply to a Christian friend's inquiry, that he has nothing to repent of. "The power which circumstances placed in my hands," he says, "and which is an emanation of divinity, I am conscious of having used to the best of my skill. I have never wittingly wronged anyone. If some should think that I have not fulfilled all expectations, they should in justice reflect that there is a mysterious power outside us, which in a great measure governs the issue of human undertakings." He still does not see eye to eye with Maximus, though there is a flash of insight in his remark to him, when he learns that the village where he fell is called the Phrygian region, that "the world-will has laid an ambush for him." It was something for Julian to have seen that the power which he found stronger than his individual will was itself will; but inasmuch as he conceived it, not as the whole of which his will was but a part, but as a rival will, he was not the man to found the third empire. He had felt the godhead in himself, but not in others. Being only able to say, with half conviction, "The kingdom of heaven is within ME," he had been utterly vanquished by the Galilean who had been able to say, "The kingdom of heaven is within YOU." But he was on the way to that full truth. A man cannot believe in others until he believes in himself; for his conviction of the equal worth of his fellows must be filled by the overflow of his conviction of his own worth. Against the spurious Christianity of asceticism, starving that indispensable prior conviction, Julian rightly rebelled ; and Maximus rightly incited him to rebel. But Maximus could not fill the prior conviction even to fulness, much less to overflowing ; for the third empire was not yet, and is not yet. Still the tyrant dies with a peaceful conscience, and Maximus is able to tell the priest at the bedside that the world-will shall answer for Julian's soul. What troubles the mystic is his having misled Julian by encouraging him to bring upon himself the fate of Cain and Judas. As water can be boiled by fire, man can be prompted and stimulated from without to assert his individuality ; but just as no boiling can fill a half-empty well, no external stimulus can enlarge the spirit of man to the point at which he can self-beget the Emperor-God in himself by willing. At that point "to will is to have to will" ; and it is with these words on his lips that Maximus leaves the stage, still sure that the third empire is to come.

It is not necessary to translate the scheme of *Emperor and Galilean* into terms of the antithesis between idealism and realism. Julian, in this respect, is a reincarnation of Peer Gynt. All the difference is that the subject which was instinctively projected in the earlier poem, is intellectually constructed as well in the later history, Julian plus Maximus the Mystic being Peer plus one who understands him better than Ibsen did when he created him. The current interest of Ibsen's interpretation of original Christianity is obvious. The deepest sayings recorded in the gospels are now nothing but eccentric paradoxes to most of those who reject the superstitious view of Christ's divinity. Those who accept that view often consider that such acceptance absolves them from attaching any sensible meaning to his words at all, and so might as well pin their faith to a stock or stone. Of these attitudes the first is superficial, and the second stupid. Ibsen's interpretation, whatever may be its validity, will certainly hold the field long after the current "Crosstianity," as it has been aptly called, becomes unthinkable.

Ibsen had now written three immense dramas, all dealing with the effect of idealism on individual egotists of exceptional imaginative excitability. This he was able to do whilst his intellectual consciousness of his theme was yet incomplete, by simply portraying sides of himself. He has put himself into the skin of Brand, of Peer Gynt, and of Julian, and these figures have accordingly a certain direct vitality which belongs to none of his subsequent creations of the male sex. There are flashes of it in Relling, in Lovborg, in Ellida's stranger from the sea; but they are only flashes: henceforth all his really vivid and solar figures are women For, having at last completed his intellectual analysis of idealism, he could now construct methodical illustrations of its social working, instead of, as before, blindly projecting imaginary personal experiences which he himself had not yet succeeded in interpreting. Further, now that he understood the matter, he could see plainly the effect of idealism as a social force on people quite unlike himself: that is to say, on everyday people in everyday life—on shipbuilders, bank managers, parsons, and doctors, as well as on saints, romantic adventurers, and emperors. With his eyes thus opened, instances of the mischief of idealism crowded upon him so rapidly that he began deliberately to inculcate their moral by writing realistic prose plays of modern life, abandoning all production of art for art's sake. His skill as a playwright and his genius as an artist were thenceforth used only to secure attention and effectiveness for his detailed attack on idealism. No more verse, no more tragedy for the sake of tears or comedy for the sake of laughter, no more seeking to produce specimens of art forms in order that literary critics might fill the public belly with the east wind. The critics, it is true, soon declared that he had ceased to be an artist; but he, having something else to do with his talent than to fulfil critics' definitions, took no notice of them, not thinking their ideal sufficiently important to write a play about.

THE LEAGUE OF YOUTH.

The first of the series of realistic prose plays is called *Pillars of Society*, but before describing this, a word must be said about a previous work which seems to have determined the form which the later series took. Between *Peer Gynt* and *Emperor and Galilean*, Ibsen had let fall an amusing comedy called *The League of Youth* (*De Unges Forbund*) in which the imaginative egotist reappears farcically as an ambitious young lawyer-politician who, smarting under a snub from a local landowner and county magnate, relieves his feelings with such a passionate explosion of Radical eloquence that he is cheered to the echo by the progressive party. Intoxicated with this success, he imagines himself a great leader of the people and a wielder of the mighty engine of democracy. He narrates to a friend a dream in which he saw kings swept helplessly over the surface of the earth by a mighty wind. He has hardly achieved this impromptu when he receives an invitation to dine with the local magnate, whose friends, to spare his feelings, have misled him as to the person aimed at in the new demagogue's speech. The invitation sets the egotist's imagination on the opposite tack: he is presently pouring forth his soul in the magnate's drawing-room to the very friend to whom he related the great dream.

"My goal is this . in the course of time I shall get into Parliament, perhaps into the Ministry, and marry happily into a rich and honourable family. I intend to reach it by my own exertions. I must and shall reach it without help from anyone. Meanwhile I shall enjoy life here, drinking in beauty and sunshine. Here there are fine manners life moves gracefully here : the very floors seem laid to be trodden only by lacquered shoes : the arm chairs are deep ; and the ladies sink exquisitely into them Here the conversation goes lightly and elegantly, like a game at battledore ; and no blunders come plumping in to make an awkward silence Here I feel for the first time what distinction means. Yes ; we have indeed an aristocracy of culture ; and to it I will belong Dont you yourself feel the refining influence of the place," &c. &c.

For the rest, the play is an ingenious comedy of intrigue, clever enough in its mechanical construction to entitle the French to claim that Ibsen owes something to his technical education as a playwright in the school of Scribe, although it is hardly necessary to add that the difference between *The League of Youth* and the typical "well made play" of Scribe is like the difference between a human being and a marionette One or two episodes in the last two acts contain the

Pillars of Society. 75

germs of later plays; and it was the suitability of the realistic prose comedy form to these episodes that no doubt confirmed Ibsen in his choice of it. Therefore *The League of Youth* would stand as the first of the realistic plays in any classification which referred to form alone. In a classification by content, with which we are here alone concerned, it must stand in its chronological place as a farcical member of the group of heroic plays beginning with *The Pretenders* and ending with *Emperor and Galilean*.

PILLARS OF SOCIETY.

Pillars of Society, then, is the first play in which Ibsen writes as one who has intellectually mastered his own didactic purpose, and no longer needs to project himself into his characters. It is the history of one Karsten Bernick, a "pillar of society" who, in pursuance of the duty of maintaining the respectability of his father's famous firm of shipbuilders (to shatter which would be to shatter one of the ideals of commercial society and to bring abstract respectability into disrepute), has averted a disgraceful exposure by allowing another man to bear the discredit not only of a love affair in which he himself had been the sinner, but of a theft which was never committed at all, having been merely alleged as an excuse for the firm being out of funds at a critical period. Bernick is an abject slave to the idealizings of a certain schoolmaster Rörlund about respectability, duty to society, good example, social influence, health of the community, and so on. When he falls in love with a married actress, he feels that no man has a right to shock the feelings of Rorlund and the community for his own selfish gratification? However, a clandestine intrigue will shock nobody, since nobody need know of it He accordingly adopts this method of satisfying himself and preserving the moral tone of the community at the same time. Unluckily, the intrigue is all but discovered; and Bernick has either to see the moral security of the community shaken to its foundations by the terrible scandal of his exposure, or else to deny what he did and put it on another man. As the other man happens to be going to America, where he can easily conceal his imputed shame, Bernick's conscience tells him that it would be little short of a crime against society to neglect such an opportunity; and he accordingly lies his way back into the good opinion of Rörlund and company at the emigrant's expense. There are three women in the play for whom the schoolmaster's ideals have no attractions. First, there is the actress's daughter, who wants to get to America because she hears that people there are not good;

and she is heartily tired of good people, since it is part of their goodness to look down on her because of her mother's disgrace. The schoolmaster, to whom she is engaged, condescends to her for the same reason. The second has already sacrified her happiness and wasted her life in conforming to Mr Stead's ideal of womanliness; and she earnestly advises the younger woman not to commit that folly, but to break her engagement with the schoolmaster, and elope promptly with the man she loves. The third is a naturally free woman who has snapped her fingers at the current ideals all her life; and it is her presence that at last encourages the liar to break with the ideals by telling the truth about himself. The comic personage of the piece is a useless hypochondriac whose function in life, as described by himself, is "to hold up the banner of the ideal." This he does by sneering at everything and everybody for not resembling the heroic incidents and characters he reads about in novels and tales of adventure. But in his obvious peevishness and folly, he is much less dangerous than the pious idealist, the earnest and respectable Rorlund. The play concludes with Bernick's admission that the spirits of Truth and Freedom are the true pillars of society, a phrase which sounds so like an idealistic commonplace that it is necessary to add that Truth in this passage does not mean the nursery convention of truth-telling satirized by Ibsen himself in a later play, as well as by Labiche and other comic dramatists. It means the unflinching recognition of facts, and the abandonment of the conspiracy to ignore such of them as do not bolster up the ideals. The idealist rule as to truth dictates the recognition only of those facts or idealistic masks of facts which have a respectable air, and the mentioning of these on all occasions and at all hazards. Ibsen urges the recognition of all facts; but as to mentioning them, he wrote a whole play, as we shall see presently, to shew that you must do that at your own peril, and that a truth-teller who cannot hold his tongue on occasion may do as much mischief as a whole university full of trained liars The word Freedom, I need hardly say, means freedom from slavery to the Rörlund ideals.

A DOLL'S HOUSE.

Unfortunately, *Pillars of Society*, as a propagandist play, is disabled by the circumstance that the hero, being a fraudulent hypocrite in the ordinary police-court sense of the phrase, is not accepted as a typical pillar of society by the class which he represents. Accordingly, Ibsen took care next time to make his idealist irreproachable from the standpoint of the ordinary idealist morality. In the famous *Doll's House*, the pillar of society who owns the doll is a model husband, father, and citizen. In his little household, with the three darling children and the affectionate little wife, all on the most loving terms with one another, we have the sweet home, the womanly woman, the happy family life of the idealist's dream. Mrs Nora Helmer is happy in the belief that she has attained a valid realization of all these illusions—that she is an ideal wife and mother, and that Helmer is an ideal husband who would, if the necessity arose, give his life to save her reputation. A few simply contrived incidents disabuse her effectually on all these points. One of her earliest acts of devotion to her husband has been the secret raising of a sum of money to enable him to make a tour which was necessary to restore his health. As he would have broken down sooner than go into debt, she has had to persuade him that the money was a gift from her father. It was really obtained from a moneylender, who refused to make her the loan unless she induced her father to endorse the promissory note. This being impossible, as her father was dying at the time, she took the shortest way out of the difficulty by writing the name herself, to the entire satisfaction of the moneylender, who, though not at all duped, knows that forged bills are often the surest to be paid. Then she slaves in secret at scrivener's work until she has nearly paid off the debt. At this point Helmer is made manager of the bank in which he is employed; and the moneylender, wishing to obtain a post there, uses the forged bill to force Nora to exert her influence with Helmer on his behalf. But she, having a hearty contempt for the man, cannot be persuaded by him that there was any harm in putting her father's name on the bill, and ridicules the suggestion that the law would not recognize that she was right under the circumstances. It is her husband's own contemptuous denunciation of a forgery formerly committed by the moneylender himself that destroys her self-satisfaction and opens her eyes to her ignorance of the serious business of the world to which her husband belongs—the world outside the home he shares with her. When he goes on to tell her that commercial dishonesty is generally to be traced to the influence of bad mothers, she begins to perceive that the happy way in which she plays with the children, and the care she takes to dress them nicely, are not sufficient to constitute her a fit person to train them. In order to redeem the forged bill, she resolves to borrow the balance due upon it from a friend of the family. She has learnt to coax her husband into giving her what she asks by appealing to his affection for her: that is, by playing all sorts of pretty tricks until he is wheedled into an amorous humour. This plan she has adopted without thinking about it, instinctively taking the line of least resistance with him. And now she naturally takes the same line with her husband's friend. An unexpected declaration of love from him is the result; and it at once explains to her the real nature of the domestic influence she has been so proud of. All her illusions about herself are now shattered: she sees herself as an ignorant and silly woman, a dangerous mother, and a wife kept for her husband's pleasure merely ; but she only clings the harder to her illusion about him : he is still the ideal husband who would make any sacrifice to rescue her from ruin. She resolves to kill herself rather than allow him to destroy his own career by taking the forgery on himself to save her reputation. The final disillusion comes when he, instead of at once proposing to pursue this ideal line of conduct when he hears of the forgery, naturally enough flies into a vulgar rage and heaps invective on her for disgracing him. Then she sees that their whole family life has been a fiction—their home a mere doll's house in which they have been playing at ideal husband and father, wife and mother. So she leaves him then and there in order to find out the reality of things for herself, and to gain some position not fundamentally false, refusing to see her children again until she is fit to be in charge of them, or to live with him until she and he become capable of a more honourable relation to one another than that in which they have hitherto stood. He at first cannot understand what has happened, and flourishes the shattered ideals over her as if they were as potent as ever. He presents the course most agreeable to him—that of her staying at home and avoiding a scandal—as her duty to her husband, to her children, and to her religion; but the magic of these disguises is gone; and at last even he understands what has really happened, and sits down alone to wonder whether that more honourable relation can ever come to pass between them.

GHOSTS.

In his next play, Ibsen returned to the charge with such an uncompromising and outspoken attack on marriage as a useless sacrifice of human beings to an ideal, that his meaning was obscured by its very obviousness. *Ghosts*, as it is called, is the story of a woman who has faithfully acted as a model wife and mother, sacrificing herself at every point with selfless thoroughness. Her husband is a man with a huge capacity and appetite for sensuous enjoyment Society, prescribing ideal duties and not enjoyment for him, drives him to enjoy himself in underhand and illicit ways When he marries his model wife, her devotion to duty only makes life harder for him ; and he at last takes refuge in the caresses of an undutiful but pleasure-loving housemaid, and leaves his wife to satisfy her conscience by managing his business affairs whilst he satisfies his cravings as best he can by reading novels, drinking, and flirting, as aforesaid, with the servants. At this point even those who are most indignant with Nora Helmer for walking out of the doll's house, must admit that Mrs Alving would be justified in walking out of *her* house But Ibsen is determined to show you what comes of the scrupulous line of conduct you were so angry with Nora for not pursuing. Mrs Alving feels that her place is by her husband for better for worse, and by her child. Now the ideal of wifely and womanly duty which demands this from her also demands that she should regard herself as an outraged wife, and her husband as a scoundrel. The family ideal again requires that she should suffer in silence, and, for her son's sake, never shatter his faith in the purity of home life by letting him know the truth about his father. It is her duty to conceal that truth from the world and from him. In this she only falters for one moment. Her marriage has not been a love match: she has, in pursuance of her duty as a daughter, contracted it for the sake of her family, although her heart inclined to a highly respectable clergyman, a professor of her own idealism, named Manders. In the humiliation of her first discovery of her husband's infidelity, she leaves the house and takes refuge with Manders; but he at once leads her back to the path of duty, from which she does not again swerve. With the utmost devotion she now carries out a tremendous scheme of lying and imposture. She so manages her husband's affairs and so shields his good name that everybody believes him to be a public-spirited citizen of the strictest conformity to current ideals of respectability and family life. She sits up of nights listening to his lewd and silly conversation, and even drinking with him, to keep him from going into the streets and betraying what she considers his vices. She provides for the servant he has seduced, and brings up his illegitimate daughter as a maid in her own household. And as a crowning sacrifice, she sends her son away to Paris to be educated there, knowing that if he stays at home the shattering of his ideals must come sooner or later. Her work is crowned with success. She gains the esteem of her old love the clergyman, who is never tired of holding up her household as a beautiful realization of the Christian ideal of marriage. Her own martyrdom is brought to an end at last by the death of her husband in the odour of a most sanctified reputation, leaving her free to recall her son from Paris and enjoy his society, and his love and gratitude, in the flower of his early manhood. But when he comes home, the facts refuse as obstinately as ever to correspond to her ideals. Oswald, the son, has inherited his father's love of enjoyment; and when, in dull rainy weather, he returns from Paris to the solemn, strictly ordered house where virtue and duty have had their temple for so many years, his mother sees him first shew the unmistakable signs of boredom with which she is so miserably familiar from of old ; then sit after dinner killing time over the bottle ; and finally — the climax of anguish— begin to flirt with the maid who, as his mother alone knows, is his own father's daughter. But there is this worldwide difference in her insight to the cases of the father and the son She did not love the father : she loves the son with the intensity of a heart-starved woman who has nothing else left to love. Instead of recoiling from him with pious disgust and Pharisaical consciousness of moral superiority, she sees at once that he has a right to be happy in his own way, and that she has no right to force him to be dutiful and wretched in hers. She sees, too, her injustice to the unfortunate father, and the iniquity of the monstrous fabric of lies and false appearances which she has wasted her life in manufacturing. She resolves that the son's life, at least, shall not be sacrificed to joyless and unnatural ideals. But she soon finds that the work of the ideals is not to be undone quite so easily. In driving the father to steal his pleasures in secrecy and squalor, they had brought upon him the diseases bred by such conditions, and her son now tells her that those diseases have left their mark on him, and that he carries poison in his pocket against the time, foretold to him by a Parisian surgeon, when he shall be struck down with softening of the brain. In desperation she turns to the task of rescuing him from this horrible apprehension by making his life happy. The house shall be made as bright as Paris for him: he shall have as much champagne as he wishes until he is no longer driven to that dangerous resource by the dulness of his life with her: if he loves the girl he shall marry her if she were fifty times his half-sister. But the half-sister, on learning the state of his health, leaves the house; for she, too, is her father's daughter, and is not going to sacrifice her life in devotion to an invalid. When the mother and son are left alone in their dreary home, with the rain still falling outside, all she can do for him is to promise that if his doom overtakes him before he can poison himself, she will make a final sacrifice of her natural feelings by performing that dreadful duty, the first of all her duties that has any real basis. Then the weather clears up at last; and the sun, which the young man has so longed to see, appears. He asks her to give it to him to play with; and a glance at him shews her that the ideals have claimed their victim, and that the time has come for her to save him from a real horror by sending him from her out of the world, just as she saved him from an imaginary one years before by sending him out of Norway.

This last scene of *Ghosts* is so appallingly tragic that the emotions it excites prevent the meaning of the play from being seized and discussed like that of *A Doll's House*. In England nobody, as far as I know, seems to have perceived that *Ghosts* is to *A Doll's House* what Mr Walter Besant intended his own "sequel"*

---

* An astonishing production, which will be found in the *English Illustrated Magazine* for January 1890. Mr Besant makes the moneylender, as a reformed man, and a pattern of all the virtues, repeat his old tactics by holding a forged bill *in terrorem* over Nora's grown-up daughter, who is engaged to his son. The bill has been to that play to be. Mr Besant attempted to shew what might come of Nora's repudiation of that idealism of which he is one of the most popular professors. But the effect made on Mr Besant by *A Doll's House* was very faint compared to that produced on the English critics by the first performance of *Ghosts* in this country. In the earlier part of this essay I have shewn that since Mrs Alving's early conceptions of duty are as valid to ordinary critics as to Pastor Manders, who must appear to them as an admirable man, endowed with Helmer's good sense without Helmer's selfishness, a pretty general disapproval of the "moral" of the play was inevitable. Fortunately, the newspaper

---

forged by her brother, who has inherited a tendency to this sort of offence from his mother. Helmer having taken to drink after the departure of his wife, and forfeited his social position, the moneylender tells the girl that if she persists in disgracing him by marrying his son, he will send her brother to gaol. She evades the dilemma by drowning herself. An exquisite absurdity is given to this *jeu d'esprit* by the moral, which is, that if Nora had never run away from her husband her daughter would never have drowned herself, and *also* by the writer's naive unconsciousness of the fact that he has represented the moneylender as doing over again what he did in the play, with the difference that, having become eminently respectable, he has also become a remorseless scoundrel. Ibsen shows him as a good-natured fellow at bottom.

press went to such bedlamite lengths on this occasion that Mr William Archer, the well-known dramatic critic and translator of Ibsen, was able to put the whole body of hostile criticism out of court by simply quoting its excesses in an article entitled *Ghosts and Gibberings*, which appeared in the *Pall Mall Gazette* of the 8th of April 1891. Mr Archer's extracts, which he offers as a nucleus for a Dictionary of Abuse modelled upon the Wagner "Schimpf-Lexicon," are worth reprinting here as samples of contemporary idealist criticism of the drama.

Descriptions of the Play.

"Ibsen's positively abominable play entitled *Ghosts*. . . This disgusting representation . . Reprobation due to such as aim at infecting the modern theatre with poison after desperately inoculating themselves and others. . An open drain; a loathsome sore unbandaged; a dirty act done publicly; a lazar-house with all its doors and windows open. . . Candid foulness . . . Kotzebue turned bestial and cynical. Offensive cynicism. . . Ibsen's melancholy and malodorous world. . . Absolutely loathsome and fetid. . Gross, almost putrid indecorum. . . . Literary carrion. . . Crapulous stuff. . . Novel and perilous nuisance."—*Daily Telegraph* (leading article). "This mass of vulgarity, egotism, coarseness, and absurdity "— *Daily Telegraph* (criticism). "Unutterably offensive. . . . Prosecution under Lord Campbell's Act. . . Abominable piece. . . Scandalous."—*Standard*. "Naked loathsomeness. . . Most dismal and repulsive production"—*Daily News* "Revoltingly suggestive and blasphemous. . . Characters either contradictory in themselves, uninteresting or abhorrent." — *Daily Chronicle*. "A repulsive and degrading work."— *Queen*. "Morbid, unhealthy, unwholesome and disgusting story. . . A piece to bring the stage into disrepute and dishonour with every right-thinking man and woman."—*Lloyd's* "Merely dull dirt long drawn out."—*Hawk*. "Morbid horrors of the hideous tale. . . Ponderous dulness of the didactic talk. . . If any repetition of this outrage be attempted, the authorities will doubtless wake from their lethargy." — *Sporting and Dramatic News*. "Just a wicked nightmare."—*The Gentlewoman*. "Lugubrious diagnosis of sordid impropriety. . . Characters are prigs, pedants, and profligates. . Morbid caricatures. . . Maunderings of nookshotten Norwegians. . . It is no more of a play than an average Gaiety burlesque."— W. St Leger in *Black and White*. "Most loathsome of all Ibsen's plays . . Garbage and offal."—*Truth* "Ibsen's putrid play called *Ghosts*. . . So loathsome an enterprise."—*Academy*. "As foul and filthy a concoction as has ever been allowed to disgrace the boards of an English theatre... Dull and disgusting... Nastiness and malodorousness laid on thickly as with a trowel."—*Era*. "Noisome corruption."—*Stage*.

Descriptions of Ibsen.

"An egotist and a bungler."—*Daily Telegraph*. "A crazy fanatic... A crazy, cranky being... Not only consistently dirty but deplorably dull."—*Truth*. "The Norwegian pessimist *in petto*" [*sic*].—W. St Leger in *Black and White*. "Ugly, nasty, discordant, and downright dull... A gloomy sort of ghoul, bent on groping for horrors by night, and blinking like a stupid old owl when the warm sunlight of the best of life dances into his wrinkled eyes."—*Gentlewoman*. "A teacher of the æstheticism of the Lock Hospital."—*Saturday Review*.

Descriptions of Ibsen's Admirers.

"Lovers of prurience and dabblers in impropriety who are eager to gratify their illicit tastes under the pretence of art."—*Evening Standard*. "Ninety-seven per cent. of the people who go to see *Ghosts* are nasty-minded people who find the discussion of nasty subjects to their taste in exact proportion to their nastiness." — *Sporting and Dramatic News.* " The sexless... The unwomanly woman, the unsexed females, the whole army of unprepossessing cranks in petticoats... Educated and muck-ferreting dogs... Effeminate men and male women... They all of them—men and women alike—know that they are doing not only a nasty but an illegal thing... The Lord Chamberlain left them alone to wallow in *Ghosts.* .. Outside a silly clique, there is not the slightest interest in the Scandinavian humbug or all his works... A wave of human folly."—*Truth.*

AN ENEMY OF THE PEOPLE.

After this, the reader will understand the temper in which Ibsen set about his next play, *An Enemy of the People*, in which, having done sufficient execution among the ordinary social, domestic, and puritanic ideals, he puts his finger for a moment on political ideals. The play deals with a local majority of middle-class people who are pecuniarily interested in concealing the fact that the famous baths which attract visitors to their town and customers to their shops and hotels are contaminated by sewage. When an honest doctor insists on exposing this danger, the townspeople immediately disguise themselves ideally. Feeling the disadvantage of appearing in their true character as a conspiracy of interested rogues against an honest man, they pose as Society, as The People, as Democracy, as the solid Liberal Majority, and other imposing abstractions, the doctor, in attacking them, of course being thereby made an enemy of The People, a danger to Society, a traitor to Democracy, an apostate from the great Liberal party, and so on. Only those who take an active part in politics can appreciate the grim fun of the situation, which, though it has an intensely local Norwegian air, will be at once recognized as typical in England, not, perhaps, by the professional literary critics, who are for the most part *fainéants* as far as political life is concerned, but certainly by everyone who has got as far as a seat on the committee of the most obscure caucus

As *An Enemy of the People* contains one or two references to democracy which are anything but respectful, it is necessary to define Ibsen's criticism of it with precision. Democracy is really only an arrangement by which the whole people are given a certain share in the control of the government. It has never been proved that this is ideally the best arrangement: it became necessary because the people willed to have it; and it has been made effective only to the very limited extent short of which the dissatisfaction of the majority would have taken the form of actual violence. Now when men had to submit to kings, they consoled themselves by making it an article of faith that the king was always right—idealized him as a Pope, in fact. In the same way we who have to submit to majorities set up Voltaire's pope, "Monsieur Tout-le-monde," and make it blasphemy against Democracy to deny that the majority is always right, although that, as Ibsen says, is a lie. It is a scientific fact that the majority, however eager it may be for the reform of old abuses, is always wrong in its opinion of new developments, or rather is always unfit for them (for it can hardly be said to be wrong in opposing developments for which it is not yet fit) The pioneer is a tiny minority of the force he heads; and so, though it is easy to be in a minority and yet be wrong, it is absolutely impossible to be in the majority and yet be right as to the newest social prospects. We should never progress at all if it were possible for each of us to stand still on democratic principles until we saw whither all the rest were moving, as our statesmen declare themselves bound to do when they are called upon to lead. Whatever clatter we may make for a time with our filing through feudal serf collars and kicking off rusty capitalistic fetters, we shall never march a step forward except at the heels of "the strongest man, he who is able to stand alone" and to turn his back on "the damned compact Liberal majority." All of which is no disparagement of adult suffrage, payment of members, annual parliaments and so on, but simply a wholesome reduction of them to their real place in the social economy as pure machinery—machinery which has absolutely no principles except the principles of mechanics, and no motive power in itself whatsoever The idealization of public organizations is as dangerous as that of kings or priests. We need to be reminded that though there is in the world a vast number of buildings in which a certain ritual is conducted before crowds called congregations by a functionary called a priest, who is subject to a central council controlling all such functionaries on a few points, there is not therefore any such thing in reality as the ideal Catholic Church, nor ever was, nor ever will be. There may, too, be a highly elaborate organization of public affairs; but there is no such thing as the ideal State. All abstractions invested with collective consciousness or collective authority, set above the individual, and exacting duty from him on pretence of acting or thinking with greater validity than he, are man-eating idols red with human sacrifices. This position must not be confounded with Anarchism, or the idealization of the repudiation of Governments. Ibsen does not refuse to pay the tax collector, but may be supposed to regard him, not as an emissary of something that does not exist and never did, called THE STATE, but simply as the man sent round by the committee of citizens (mostly fools as far as "the third empire" is concerned) to collect the money for the police or the paving and lighting of the streets

THE WILD DUCK.

After *An Enemy of the People*, Ibsen, as I have said, left the vulgar ideals for dead, and set about the exposure of those of the choicer spirits, beginning with the incorrigible idealists who had idealized his very self, and were becoming known as Ibsenites. His first move in this direction was such a tragi-comic slaughtering of sham Ibsenism that his astonished victims plaintively declared that *The Wild Duck*, as the new play was called, was a satire on his former works; whilst the pious, whom he had disappointed so severely by his interpretation of *Brand*, began to think that he had come back repentant to the fold. The household to which we are introduced in *The Wild Duck* is not, like Mrs Alving's, a handsome one made miserable by superstitious illusions, but a shabby one made happy by romantic illusions. The only member of it who sees it as it really is is the wife, a good-

The Wild Duck.

natured Philistine who desires nothing better. The husband, a vain, petted, spoilt dawdler, believes that he is a delicate and high-souled man, devoting his life to redeeming his old father's name from the disgrace brought on it by an imprisonment for breach of the forest laws. This redemption he proposes to effect by making himself famous as a great inventor some day when he has the necessary inspiration. Their daughter, a girl in her teens, believes intensely in her father and in the promised invention. The disgraced grandfather cheers himself by drink whenever he can get it; but his chief resource is a wonderful garret full of rabbits and pigeons. The old man has procured a number of second-hand Christmas trees; and with these he has turned the garret into a sort of toy forest, in which he can play at bear hunting, which was one of the sports of his youth and prosperity. The weapons employed in the hunting expeditions are a gun which will not go off, and a pistol which occasionally brings down a rabbit or a pigeon. A crowning touch is given to the illusion by a wild duck, which, however, must not be shot, as it is the special property of the girl, who reads and dreams whilst the woman cooks and washes, besides carrying on the photographic work which is supposed to be the business of her husband. She does not appreciate his highly strung sensitiveness of character, which is constantly suffering agonizing jars from her vulgarity; but then she does not appreciate that other fact that he is a lazy and idle impostor. Downstairs there is a disgraceful clergyman named Molvik, a hopeless drunkard; but even he respects himself and is tolerated because of a special illusion invented for him by another lodger, a doctor—the now famous Dr Relling—upon whom the lesson of the household above has not been thrown away. Molvik, says the doctor, must break out into drinking fits because he is daimonic, an interesting explanation which completely relieves the reverend gentleman from the imputation of vulgar tippling.

Into this domestic circle there comes a new lodger, an idealist of the most advanced type. He greedily swallows the daimonic theory of the clergyman's drunkenness, and enthusiastically accepts the photographer as the high-souled hero he supposes himself to be; but he is troubled because the relations of the man and his wife do not constitute an ideal marriage. He happens to know that the woman, before her marriage, was the cast-off mistress of his own father; and because she has not told her husband this, he conceives her life as founded on a lie, like that of Bernick in *Pillars of Society*. He accordingly sets himself to work out the woman's salvation for her, and establish ideally frank relations between the pair, by simply blurting out the truth, and then asking them, with fatuous self-satisfaction, whether they do not feel much the better for it. This wanton piece of mischief has more serious results than a mere domestic scene. The husband is too weak to act on his bluster about outraged honour and the impossibility of his ever living with his wife again; and the woman is merely annoyed with the idealist for telling on her; but the girl takes the matter to heart and shoots herself. The doubt cast on her parentage, with her father's theatrical repudiation of her, destroy her ideal place in the home, and make her a source of discord there; so she sacrifices herself, thereby carrying out the teaching of the idealist mischief-maker, who has talked a good deal to her about the duty and beauty of self-sacrifice, without foreseeing that he might be taken in mortal earnest. The busybody thus finds that people cannot be freed from their failings from without. They must free themselves. When Nora is strong enough to live out of the doll's house, she will go out of it of her own accord if the door stands open; but if before that period you take her by the scruff of the neck and thrust her out, she will only take refuge in the next establishment of the kind that offers to receive her. Woman has thus two enemies to deal with : the old-fashioned one who wants to keep the door locked, and the new-fashioned one who wants to thrust her into the street before she is ready to go. In the cognate case of a hypocrite and liar like Bernick, exposing him is a mere police measure he is none the less a liar and hypocrite when you have exposed him. If you want to make a sincere and truthful man of him, all that you can do is to remove what you can of the external obstacles to his exposing himself, and then wait for the operation of his internal impulse to confess. If he has no such impulse, then you must put up with him as he is. It is useless to make claims on him which he is not yet prepared to meet. Whether, like Brand, we make such claims because to refrain would be to compromise with evil, or, like Gregers Werle, because we think their moral beauty must recommend them at sight to every one, we shall alike incur Relling's impatient assurance that "life would be quite tolerable if we could only get rid of the confounded duns that keep on pestering us in our poverty with the claims of the ideal"

ROSMERSHOLM.

Ibsen did not in *The Wild Duck* exhaust the subject of the danger of forming ideals for other people, and interfering in their lives with a view to enabling them to realize those ideals. Cases far more typical than that of the meddlesome lodger are those of the priest who regards the ennobling of mankind as a sort of trade process of which his cloth gives him a monopoly, and the clever woman who pictures a noble career for the man she loves, and devotes herself to helping him to achieve it. In *Rosmersholm*, the play with which Ibsen followed up *The Wild Duck*, there is an unpractical country parson, a gentleman of ancient stock, whose family has been for many years a centre of social influence. The tradition of that influence reinforces his priestly tendency to regard the ennoblement of the world as an external operation to be performed by himself; and the need of such ennoblement is very evident to him; for his nature is a fine one: he looks at the world with some dim prevision of "the third empire." He is married to a woman of passionately affectionate nature, who is very fond of him, but does not regard him as a regenerator of the human race. Indeed she does not share any of his dreams, and only acts as an extinguisher on the sacred fire of his idealism. He, she, her brother Kroll the headmaster, Kroll's wife, and their set form a select circle of the best people in the place, comfortably orbited in the social system, and quite planetary in ascertained position and unimpeachable respectability Into the orbit comes presently a wandering star, one Rebecca Gamvik, an unpropertied orphan, who has been allowed to read advanced books, and is a Freethinker and a Radical—all things that disqualify a poor woman for admission to the Rosmer world. However, one must live somewhere, and as the Rosmer world is the only one in which an ambitious and cultivated woman can find powerful allies and educated companions, Rebecca, being both ambitious and cultivated, makes herself agreeable to the Rosmer circle with such success that the affectionate and impulsive but unintelligent Mrs Rosmer becomes wildly fond of her, and is not content until she has persuaded her to come and live with them. Rebecca, then a mere adventuress fighting for a foothold in polite society (which has hitherto shown itself highly indignant at her thrusting herself in where nobody has thought of providing room for her), accepts the offer all the more readily because she has taken the measure of Parson Rosmer, and formed the idea of playing upon his aspirations, and making herself a leader in politics and society by using him as a figure-head

But now two difficulties arise First, there is Mrs Rosmer's extinguishing effect on her husband—an effect which convinces Rebecca that nothing can be done with him whilst his wife is in the way. Second—a contingency quite unallowed for in her provident calculations—she finds herself passionately enamoured of him. The poor parson, too, falls in love with her; but he does not know it. He turns to the woman who understands him like a sunflower to the sun, and makes her his real friend and companion. The wife feels this soon enough; and he, quite unconscious of it, begins to think that her mind must be affected, since she has become so intensely miserable and hysterical about nothing—nothing that he can see. The truth is that she has come under the curse of the ideal too : she sees herself standing, a useless obstacle, between her husband and the woman he really loves, the woman who can help him to a glorious career. She cannot even be the mother in the household ; for she is childless. Then comes Rebecca, fortified with a finely reasoned theory that Rosmer's future is staked against his wife's life, and says that it is better for all their sakes that she should quit Rosmersholm. She even hints that she must go at once if a grave scandal is to be avoided. Mrs Rosmer, regarding a scandal in Rosmersholm as the most terrible thing that can happen, and seeing that it could be averted by the marriage of Rebecca and Rosmer if she were out of the way, writes a letter secretly to Rosmer's bitterest enemy, the editor of the local Radical paper, a man who has forfeited his moral reputation by an intrigue which Rosmer has pitilessly denounced. In this letter she implores him not to believe or publish any stories that he may hear about Rosmer, to the effect that he is in any way to blame for anything that may happen to her. Then she sets Rosmer free to marry Rebecca, and to realize his ideals, by going out into the garden and throwing herself into the millstream that runs there.

Now follows a period of quiet mourning at Rosmersholm. Everybody except Rosmer suspects that Mrs Rosmer was not mad, and guesses why she committed suicide. Only it would not do to compromise the aristocratic party by treating Rosmer as the Radical editor was treated. So the neighbours shut their eyes and condole with the bereaved clergyman; and the Radical editor holds his tongue because Radicalism is getting respectable, and he hopes, with Rebecca's help, to get Rosmer over to his side presently. Meanwhile the unexpected has again happened to Rebecca. Her passion is worn out; but in the long days of mourning she has found the higher love; and it is now for Rosmer's own sake that she urges him to become a man of action, and brood no more over the dead. When his friends start a Conservative paper and ask him to become editor, she induces him to reply by declaring himself a Radical and Freethinker. To his utter amazement, the result is, not an animated discussion of his views, but just such an attack on his home life and private conduct as he had formerly made on those of the Radical editor. His friends tell him plainly that the compact of silence is broken by his defection, and that there will be no mercy for the traitor to the party. Even the Radical editor not only refuses to publish the fact that his new ally is a Freethinker (which would destroy all his social weight as a Radical recruit), but brings up the dead woman's letter as a proof that the attack is sufficiently well-founded to make it unwise to go too far. Rosmer, who at first had been simply shocked that men whom he had always honoured as gentlemen should descend to such hideous calumny, now sees that he really did love Rebecca, and is indeed guilty of his wife's death. His first impulse is to shake off the spectre of the dead woman by marrying Rebecca ; but she, knowing that the guilt is hers, puts that temptation behind her and refuses. Then, as he thinks it all over, his dream of ennobling the world slips away from him . such work can only be done by a man conscious of his own innocence. To save him from despair,

Rebecca makes a great sacrifice She "gives him back his innocence" by confessing how she drove his wife to kill herself; and, as the confession is made in the presence of Kroll, she ascribes the whole plot to her ambition, and says not a word of her passion Rosmer, confounded as he realizes what helpless puppets they have all been in the hands of this clever woman, for the moment misses the point that unscrupulous ambition, though it explains her crime, does not account for her confession. He turns his back on her and leaves the house with Kroll. She quietly packs up her trunk, and is about to vanish from Rosmersholm without another word when he comes back alone to ask why she confessed. She tells him why, offering him her self-sacrifice as a proof that his power of ennobling others was no vain dream, since it is his companionship that has changed her from the selfish adventuress she was to the devoted woman she has just proved herself to be. But he has lost his faith in himself, and cannot believe her. The proof is too subtle, too artful: he cannot forget that she duped him by flattering this very weakness of his before. Besides, he knows now that it is not true—that people are not ennobled from without. She has no more to say; for she can think of no further proof. But he has thought of an unanswerable one. Dare she make all doubt impossible by doing for his sake what the wife did ? She asks what would happen if she had the heart and the will to do it. " Then," he replies, " I should have to believe in you I should recover my faith in my mission. Faith in my power to ennoble human souls Faith in the human soul's power to attain nobility " " You shall have your faith again," she answers. At this pass the inner truth of the situation comes out ; and the thin veil of a demand for " proof", with its monstrous sequel of asking the woman to kill herself in order to restore the man's good opinion of himself, falls away. What has really seized Rosmer is the old fatal ideal of expiation by sacrifice. He sees that when Rebecca goes into the millstream he must go too. And he speaks his real mind in the words, " There is no judge over us : therefore we must do justice upon ourselves." But the woman's soul is free of this to the end , for when she says, " I am under the power of the Rosmersholm view of life *now* What I have sinned it is fit I should expiate," we feel in that speech a protest against the Rosmersholm view of life—the view that denied her right to live and be happy from the first, and now at the end, even in denying its God, exacts her life as a vain blood-offering for its own blindness. The woman has the higher light : she goes to her death out of fellowship with the man who is driven thither by the superstition which has destroyed his will. The story ends with his taking her solemnly as his wife, and casting himself with her into the millstream.

It is unnecessary to repeat here what is said on page 36 as to the vital part played in this drama by the evolution of the lower into the higher love. Peer Gynt, during the prophetic episode in his career, shocks the dancing girl Anitra into a remonstrance by comparing himself to a cat. He replies, with his wisest air, that from the standpoint of love there is perhaps not so much difference between a tomcat and a prophet as she may imagine. The number of critics who have entirely missed the point of Rebecca's transfiguration seems to indicate that the majority of men, even among critics of dramatic poetry, have not got beyond Peer Gynt's opinion in this matter. No doubt they would not endorse it as a definitely stated proposition, aware, as they are, that there is a poetic convention to the contrary. But if they fail to recognize the only possible alternative proposition when it is not only stated in so many words by Rebecca West, but when without it her conduct dramatically contradicts her character—when they even complain of the contradiction as a blemish on the play, I am afraid there can be no further doubt that the extreme perplexity into which the first performance of *Rosmersholm* in England plunged the Press was due entirely to the prevalence of Peer Gynt's view of love among the dramatic critics.

THE LADY FROM THE SEA.

Ibsen's next play, though it deals with the old theme, does not insist on the power of ideals to kill, as the two previous plays do. It rather deals with the origin of ideals in unhappiness— in dissatisfaction with the real The subject of *The Lady from the Sea* is the most poetic fancy imaginable. A young woman, brought up on the sea-coast, marries a respectable doctor, a widower, who idolizes her and places her in his household with nothing to do but dream and be made much of by everybody. Even the housekeeping is done by her stepdaughter · she has no responsibility, no care, and no trouble. In other words, she is an idle, helpless, utterly dependent article of luxury. A man turns red at the thought of being such a thing ; but he thoughtlessly accepts a pretty and fragile-looking woman in the same position as a charming natural picture. The lady from the sea feels an indefinite want in her life. She reads her want into all other lives, and comes to the conclusion that man once had to choose whether he would be a land animal or a creature of the sea, and that having chosen the land, he has carried about with him ever since a secret sorrow for the element he has forsaken. The dissatisfaction that gnaws her is, as she interprets it, this desperate longing for the sea. When her only child dies and leaves her without the work of a mother to give her a valid place in the world, she yields wholly to her longing, and no longer cares for her husband, who, like Rosmer, begins to fear that she is going mad. At last a seaman appears and claims her as his wife on the ground that they went years before through a rite which consisted of their marrying the sea by throwing their rings into it. This man, who had to fly from her in the old time because he killed his captain, and who fills her with a sense of dread and mystery, seems to her to embody the attraction which the sea has for her. She tells her husband that she must go away with the seaman. Naturally the doctor expostulates—declares that he cannot for her own sake let her do so mad a thing. She replies that he can only prevent her by locking her up, and asks him what satisfaction it will be to him to have her body under lock and key whilst her heart is with the other man. In vain he urges that he will only keep her under restraint until the seaman goes—that he must not, dare not, allow her to ruin herself. Her argument remains unanswerable. The seaman openly declares that she will come, so that the distracted husband asks him does he suppose he can force her from her home. To this the seaman replies that, on the contrary, unless she comes of her own free will there is no satisfaction to him in her coming at all—the unanswerable argument again. She echoes it by demanding her freedom to choose. Her husband must cry off his law-made and Church-made bargain; renounce his claim to the fulfilment of her vows; and leave her free to go back to the sea with her old lover. Then the doctor, with a heavy heart, drops his prate about his heavy responsibility for her actions, and throws the responsibility on her by crying off as she demands. The moment she feels herself a free and responsible woman, all her childish fancies vanish: the seaman becomes simply an old acquaintance whom she no longer cares for; and the doctor's affection produces its natural effect. In short, she says No to the seaman, and takes over the housekeeping keys from her stepdaughter without any further speculations concerning that secret sorrow for the abandoned sea

It should be noted here that Ellida, the Lady from the Sea, appears a much more fantastic person to English readers than to Norwegian ones. The same thing is true of many other characters drawn by Ibsen, notably Peer Gynt, who, if born in England, would certainly not have been a poet and metaphysician as well as a blackguard and a speculator. The extreme type of Norwegian, as depicted by Ibsen, imagines himself doing wonderful things, but does nothing. He dreams as no Englishman dreams, and drinks to make himself dream the more, until his effective will is destroyed, and he becomes a broken-down, disreputable sot, carrying about the tradition that he is a hero, and discussing himself on that assumption. Although the number of persons who dawdle their life away over fiction in England must be frightful, and is probably increasing, yet we have no Ulric Brendels, Rosmers, Ellidas, Peer Gynts, nor anything at all like them, and it is for this reason that I am disposed to fear that *Rosmersholm* and *The Lady from the Sea* will always be received much more incredulously by English audiences than *A Doll's House* and the plays in which the leading figures are men and women of action.

HEDDA GABLER.

Hedda Gabler, the heroine after whom the last of Ibsen's plays (so far) is named, has no ideals at all. She is a pure sceptic, a typical nineteenth century figure, falling into the abyss between the ideals which do not impose on her and the realities which she has not yet discovered. The result is that she has no heart, no courage, no conviction. With great beauty and great energy she remains mean, envious, insolent, cruel in protest against others' happiness, a bully in reaction from her own cowardice. Hedda's father, a general, is a widower. She has the traditions of the military caste about her; and these narrow her activities to the customary hunt for a socially and pecuniarily eligible husband. She makes the acquaintance of a young man of genius who, prohibited by an ideal-ridden society from taking his pleasures except where there is nothing to restrain him from excess, is going to the bad in search of his good, with the usual consequences. Hedda is intensely curious about the side of life which is forbidden to her, and in which powerful instincts, absolutely ignored and condemned by the society with which intercourse is permitted to her, steal their satisfaction. An odd intimacy springs up between the inquisitive girl and the rake. Whilst the general reads the paper in the afternoon, Lovborg and Hedda have long conversations in which he describes to her all his disreputable adventures. Although she is the questioner, she never dares to trust him: all the questions are indirect; and the responsibility for his interpretations rests on him alone. Hedda has no conviction whatever that these conversations are disgraceful, but she will not risk a fight with society on the point: hypocrisy, the homage that truth pays to falsehood, is easier to face, as far as she can see, than ostracism. When he proceeds to make advances to her, Hedda has again no conviction that it would be wrong for her to gratify his instinct and her own, so that she is confronted with the alternative of sinning against herself and him, or sinning against social ideals in which she has no faith. Making the coward's choice, she carries it out with the utmost bravado, threatening Lövborg with one of her father's pistols, and driving him out of the house with all that ostentation of outraged purity which is the instinctive defence of women to whom chastity is not natural, much as libel actions are mostly brought by persons concerning whom libels are virtually, if not technically, justifiable.

Hedda, deprived of her lover, now finds that a life of conformity without faith involves something more terrible than the utmost ostracism: to wit, boredom. This scourge, unknown among revolutionists, is the curse which makes the security of respectability as dust in the balance against the unflagging interest of rebellion, and which forces society to eke out its harmless resources for killing time by licensing gambling, gluttony, hunting, shooting, coursing, and other vicious distractions for which even idealism has no disguise. These licenses, however, are only available for people who have more than enough money to keep up appearances with; and as Hedda's father is too poor to leave her much more than the case of pistols, her boredom is only mitigated by dancing, at which she gains much admiration, but no substantial offers of marriage. At last she has to find someone to support her. A good-natured mediocrity of a professor is all that is to be had; and though she regards him as a member of an inferior class, and despises almost to loathing his family circle of two affectionate old aunts and the inevitable general servant who has helped to bring him up, she marries him *faute de mieux*, and immediately proceeds to wreck this prudent provision for her livelihood by accommodating his income to her expenditure instead of accommodating her expenditure to his income. Her nature so rebels against the whole sordid transaction that the prospect of bearing a child to her husband drives her almost frantic, since it will not only expose her to the intimate solicitude of his aunts in the course of a derangement of her health in which she can see nothing that is not repulsive and humiliating, but will make her one of his family in earnest. To amuse herself in these galling circumstances, she forms an underhand alliance with a visitor who belongs to her old set, an elderly gallant who quite understands how little she cares for her husband, and proposes a *ménage à trois* to her. She consents to his coming there and talking to her as he pleases behind her husband's back; but she keeps her pistols in reserve in case he becomes seriously importunate. He, on the other hand, tries to get some hold over her by placing her husband under pecuniary obligations, as far as he can do it without being out of pocket. And so Hedda's married life begins, with only this gallant as a precaution against the most desperate tedium.

Meanwhile Lövborg is drifting to disgrace by the nearest way—through drink. In due time he descends from lecturing at the university on the history of civilization to taking a job in an out-of-the-way place as tutor to the little children of Sheriff Elvsted. This functionary, on being left a widower with a number of children, marries their governess, finding that she will cost him less and be bound to do more for him as his wife. As for her, she is too poor to dream of refusing such a settlement in life. When Lövborg comes, his society is heaven to her. He does not dare to tell her about his dissipations; but he tells her about his unwritten books. She does not dare to remonstrate with him for drinking; but he gives it up as soon as he sees that it shocks her. Just as Mr Fearing,

Hedda Gabler. 117

in Bunyan's story, was in a way the bravest of the pilgrims, so this timid and unfortunate Mrs Elvsted trembles her way to a point at which Lövborg, quite reformed, publishes one book which makes him celebrated for the moment, and completes another, fair-copied in her handwriting, to which he looks for a solid position as an original thinker. But he cannot now stay tutoring Elvsted's children; so off he goes to town with his pockets full of the money the published book has brought him. Left once more in her old lonely plight, knowing that without her Lövborg will probably relapse into dissipation, and that without him her life will not be worth living, Mrs Elvsted is now confronted, on her own higher plane, with the same alternative which Hedda encountered. She must either sin against herself and him or against the institution of marriage under which Elvsted purchased his housekeeper. It never occurs to her even that she has any choice. She knows that her action will count as "a dreadful thing"; but she sees that she must go; and accordingly Elvsted finds himself without a wife and his children without a governess, and so disappears unpitied from the story.

Now it happens that Hedda's husband, Jörgen Tesman, is an old friend and competitor (for academic honours) of Lövborg, and also that

Hedda was a schoolfellow of Mrs Elvsted, or Thea, as she had better now be called. Thea's first business is to find out where Lovborg is; for hers is no preconcerted elopement: she has hurried to town to keep Lovborg away from the bottle, a design which she dare not hint at to himself. Accordingly, the first thing she does is to call on the Tesmans, who have just returned from their honeymoon, to beg them to invite Lövborg to their house so as to keep him in good company. They consent, with the result that the two pairs are brought together under the same roof, and the tragedy begins to work itself out

Hedda's attitude now demands a careful analysis. Lövborg's experience with Thea has enlightened his judgment of Hedda, and as he is, in his gifted way, an arrant *poseur* and male coquet, he immediately tries to get on romantic terms with her—for have they not "a past"?—by impressing her with the penetrating criticism that she is and always was a coward She admits that the virtuous heroics with the pistol were pure cowardice; but she is still so void of any other standard of conduct than conformity to the conventional ideals, that she thinks her cowardice consisted in not daring to be wicked. That is, she thinks that what she actually did was the right thing; and since she despises herself for doing it, and feels that he also rightly despises her for doing it, she gets a passionate feeling that what is wanted is the courage to do wrong. This unlooked-for reaction of idealism —this monstrous but very common setting-up of wrong-doing as an ideal, and of the wrongdoer as a hero or heroine *qua* wrongdoer — leads Hedda to conceive that when Lovborg tried to seduce her he was a hero, and that in allowing Thea to reform him he has played the recreant. In acting on this misconception, she is restrained by no consideration for any of the rest. Like all people whose lives are valueless, she has no more sense of the value of Lovborg's or Tesman's or Thea's lives than a railway shareholder has of the value of a shunter's. She gratifies her intense jealousy of Thea by deliberately taunting Lovborg into breaking loose from her influence by joining a carouse at which he not only loses his manuscript, but finally gets into the hands of the police through behaving outrageously in the house of a disreputable woman whom he accuses of stealing it, not knowing that it has been picked up by Tesman and handed to Hedda for safe keeping. Now to Hedda this bundle of paper in another woman's handwriting is the fruit of Lovborg's union with Thea he himself speaks of it as "their child." So when he turns his despair to romantic account by coming to the two women and making a tragic scene, telling Thea that he has cast the manuscript, torn into a thousand pieces, out upon the fiord ; and then, when she is gone, telling Hedda that he has brought " the child " to a house of ill-fame and lost it there, she, deceived by his posing, and thirsting to gain faith in human nobility from a heroic deed of some sort, makes him a present of one of her pistols, only begging him to " do it beautifully", by which she means that he is to kill himself without spoiling his appearance He takes it unblushingly, and leaves her with the air of a man who is looking his last on earth. But the moment he is out of sight of his audience, he goes back to the house where he still supposes that the manuscript was lost, and there renews the wrangle of the night before, using the pistol to threaten the woman, with the result that he gets shot in the abdomen, leaving the weapon to fall into the hands of the police. Meanwhile Hedda deliberately burns " the child." Then comes her elderly gallant to tell her the true story of the heroic deed which Lovborg promised her to do so beautifully, and to make her understand that he himself has now got her into his power by his ability to identify the pistol. She has either to be the slave of this man, or else to face the scandal of the connection of her name at the inquest with a squalid debauch ending in a

Hedda Gabler.

murder. Thea, too, is not crushed by Lövborg's death. Ten minutes after she has received the news with a cry of heartfelt loss, she sits down with Tesman to reconstruct "the child" from the old notes which she has preserved. Over the congenial task of collecting and arranging another man's ideas Tesman is perfectly happy, and forgets his beautiful Hedda for the first time. Thea the trembler is still mistress of the situation, holding the dead Lovborg, gaining Tesman, and leaving Hedda to her elderly admirer, who smoothly remarks that he will answer for Mrs Tesman not being bored whilst her husband is occupied with Thea in putting the pieces of the book together. However, he has again reckoned without General Gabler's second pistol. She shoots herself then and there, and so the story ends.

V.

THE MORAL OF THE PLAYS.

IN following this sketch of the plays written by Ibsen to illustrate his thesis that the real slavery of to-day is slavery to ideals of virtue, it may be that readers who have conned Ibsen through idealist spectacles have wondered that I could so pervert the utterances of a great poet. Indeed I know already that many of those who are most fascinated by the poetry of the plays will plead for any explanation of them rather than that given by Ibsen himself in the plainest terms through the mouths of Mrs Alving, Relling, and the rest. No great writer uses his skill to conceal his meaning. There is a tale by a famous Scotch story-teller which would have suited Ibsen exactly if he had hit on it first. Jeanie Deans sacrificing her sister's life on the scaffold to her own ideal of duty is far more horrible than the sacrifice in *Rosmersholm*, and the *deus ex machina* expedient by which Scott makes the end of his story agreeable is no solution of the moral problem raised, but only a

The Moral of the Plays. 123

puerile evasion of it He undoubtedly believed that it was right that Effie should hang for the sake of Jeanie's ideals * Consequently, if I were to pretend that Scott wrote *The Heart of Midlothian* to shew that people are led to do as mischievous, as unnatural, as murderous things by their religious and moral ideals as by their envy and ambition, it would be easy to confute me from the pages of the book itself. But Ibsen has made his meaning no less plain than Scott's. If any one attempts to maintain that *Ghosts* is a polemic in favour of indissoluble monogamic marriage, or that *The Wild Duck* was written to inculcate that truth should be told for its own sake, they must burn the text of the plays if their contention is to stand. The reason that Scott's story is tolerated by those who shrink from *Ghosts* is not that it is less

---

* The common-sense solution of the moral problem has often been delivered by acclamation in the theatre. Some sixteen or seventeen years ago I witnessed a performance of a melodrama founded on this story. After the painful trial scene, in which Jeanie Deans condemns her sister to death by refusing to swear to a perfectly innocent fiction, came a scene in the prison. "If it had been me," said the jailor, "I wad ha' sworn a hole through an iron pot." The roar of applause which burst from the pit and gallery was thoroughly Ibsenite in sentiment The speech, by the way, was a "gag" of the actor's, and is not to be found in the acting edition of the play.

terrible, but that Scott's views are familiar to all well-brought-up ladies and gentlemen, whereas Ibsen's are for the moment so strange as to be almost unthinkable. He is so great a poet that the idealist finds himself in the dilemma of being unable to conceive that such a genius should have an ignoble meaning, and yet equally unable to conceive his real meaning as otherwise than ignoble. Consequently he misses the meaning altogether in spite of Ibsen's explicit and circumstantial insistence on it, and proceeds to interpolate a meaning which conforms to his own ideal of nobility. Ibsen's deep sympathy with his idealist figures seems to countenance this method of making confusion. Since it is on the weaknesses of the higher types of character that idealism seizes, his examples of vanity, selfishness, folly, and failure are not vulgar villains, but men who in an ordinary novel or melodrama would be heroes. His most tragic point is reached in the destinies of Brand and Rosmer, who drive those whom they love to death in its most wanton and cruel form. The ordinary Philistine commits no such atrocities: he marries the woman he likes and lives more or less happily ever after; but that is not because he is greater than Brand or Rosmer, but because he is less The idealist is a more dangerous animal than the Philistine just as a man is a more dangerous animal than a sheep Though Brand virtually murdered his wife, I can understand many a woman, comfortably married to an amiable Philistine, reading the play and envying the victim her husband For when Brand's wife, having made the sacrifice he has exacted, tells him that he was right ; that she is happy now ; that she sees God face to face—but reminds him that "whoso sees Jehovah dies," he instinctively clasps his hands over her eyes , and that action raises him at once far above the criticism that sneers at idealism from beneath, instead of surveying it from the clear ether above, which can only be reached through its mists

If, in my account of the plays, I have myself suggested false judgments by describing the errors of the idealists in the terms of the life they had risen above rather than in that of the life they fell short of, I can only plead, with but a moderate disrespect to a large section of my readers, that if I had done otherwise I should have failed wholly to make the matter understood. Indeed the terms of the realist morality have not yet appeared in our living language , and I have already, in this very distinction between idealism and realism, been forced to insist on a sense of these terms which, had not Ibsen forced my hand, I should perhaps have conveyed otherwise, so strongly does it conflict in many of its applications with the vernacular use of the words. This, however, was a trifle compared to the difficulty which arose, when personal characters had to be described, from our inveterate habit of labelling men with the names of their moral qualities without the slightest reference to the underlying will which sets these qualities in action. At a recent anniversary celebration of the Paris Commune of 1871, I was struck by the fact that no speaker could find a eulogy for the Federals which would not have been equally appropriate to the peasants of La Vendée who fought for their tyrants against the French revolutionists, or to the Irishmen and Highlanders who fought for the Stuarts at the Boyne or Culloden. Nor could the celebrators find any other adjectives for their favourite leaders of the Commune than those which had recently been liberally applied by all the journals to an African explorer whose achievements were just then held in the liveliest abhorrence by the whole meeting. The statements that the slain members of the Commune were heroes who died for a noble ideal would have left a stranger quite as much in the dark about them as the counter statements, once common enough in middle-class newspapers, that they were incendiaries and assassins. Our obituary notices are examples of the same ambiguity. Of all the public men lately deceased, none have been made more interesting by strongly marked personal characteristics than the late Charles Bradlaugh. He was not in the least like any other notable member of the House of Commons. Yet when the obituary notices appeared, with the usual string of qualities—eloquence, determination, integrity, strong common-sense, and so on, it would have been possible, by merely expunging all names and other external details from these notices, to leave the reader entirely unable to say whether the subject of them was Mr Gladstone, Mr Morley, Mr Stead, or any one else no more like Mr Bradlaugh than Garibaldi or the late Cardinal Newman, whose obituary certificates of morality might nevertheless have been reprinted almost verbatim for the occasion without any gross incongruity. Bradlaugh had been the subject of many sorts of newspaper notice in his time. Ten years ago, when the middle classes supposed him to be a revolutionist, the string of qualities which the press hung upon him were all evil ones, great stress being laid on the fact that as he was an atheist it would be an insult to God to admit him to Parliament When it became apparent that he was a conservative force in politics, he, without any recantation of his atheism, at once had the string of evil qualities exchanged for a rosary of good ones; but it is hardly necessary to add that neither the old badge nor the new will ever give any inquirer the least clue to the sort of man he actually was: he might have been Oliver Cromwell or Wat Tyler or Jack Cade, Penn or Wilberforce or Wellington, the late Mr Hampden of flat-earth-theory notoriety or Proudhon or the Archbishop of Canterbury, for all the distinction that such labels could give him one way or the other. The worthlessness of these accounts of individuals is recognized in practice every day. Tax a stranger before a crowd with being a thief, a coward, and a liar, and the crowd will suspend its judgment until you answer the question, "What's he done?" Attempt to make a collection for him on the ground that he is an upright, fearless, high-principled hero; and the same question must be answered before a penny goes into the hat.

The reader must therefore discount those partialities which I have permitted myself to express in telling the stories of the plays. They are as much beside the mark as any other example of the sort of criticism which seeks to create an impression favourable or otherwise to Ibsen by simply pasting his characters all over with good or bad conduct marks. If any person cares to describe Hedda Gabler as a modern Lucretia who preferred death to dishonour, and Thea Elvsted as an abandoned, perjured strumpet who

The Moral of the Plays.

deserted the man she had sworn before her God to love, honour, and obey until her death, the play contains conclusive evidence establishing both points. If the critic goes on to argue that as Ibsen manifestly means to recommend Thea's conduct above Hedda's by making the end happier for her, the moral of the play is a vicious one, that, again, cannot be gainsaid If, on the other hand, *Ghosts* be defended, as the dramatic critic of *Piccadilly* lately did defend it, because it throws into divine relief the beautiful figure of the simple and pious Pastor Manders, the fatal compliment cannot be parried. When you have called Mrs Alving an "emancipated woman" or an unprincipled one, Alving a debauchee or a "victim of society," Nora a fearless and noble-hearted woman or a shocking little liar and an unnatural mother, Helmer a selfish hound or a model husband and father, according to your bias, you have said something which is at once true and false, and in either case perfectly idle.

The statement that Ibsen's plays have an immoral tendency, is, in the sense in which it is used, quite true. Immorality does not necessarily imply mischievous conduct: it implies conduct, mischievous or not, which does not conform to current ideals. Since Ibsen has devoted himself almost entirely to shewing that the spirit or will of Man is constantly outgrowing his ideals, and that therefore conformity to them is constantly producing results no less tragic than those which follow the violation of ideals which are still valid, the main effect of his plays is to keep before the public the importance of being always prepared to act immorally, to remind men that they ought to be as careful how they yield to a temptation to tell the truth as to a temptation to hold their tongues, and to urge upon women that the desirability of their preserving their chastity depends just as much on circumstances as the desirability of taking a cab instead of walking. He protests against the ordinary assumption that there are certain supreme ends which justify all means used to attain them; and insists that every end shall be challenged to shew that it justifies the means. Our ideals, like the gods of old, are constantly demanding human sacrifices. Let none of them, says Ibsen, be placed above the obligation to prove that they are worth the sacrifices they demand; and let every one refuse to sacrifice himself and others from the moment he loses his faith in the reality of the ideal. Of course it will be said here by incorrigibly slipshod readers that this, so far from being immoral, is the highest morality; and so, in a sense, it is; but I really shall not waste any further explanation on those

The Moral of the Plays. 131

who will neither mean one thing or another by a word nor allow me to do so. In short, then, among those who are not ridden by current ideals no question as to the morality of Ibsen's plays will ever arise ; and among those who are so ridden his plays will seem immoral, and cannot be defended against the accusation

There can be no question as to the effect likely to be produced on an individual by his conversion from the ordinary acceptance of current ideals as safe standards of conduct, to the vigilant open-mindedness of Ibsen It must at once greatly deepen the sense of moral responsibility. Before conversion the individual anticipates nothing worse in the way of examination at the judgment bar of his conscience than such questions as, Have you kept the commandments? Have you obeyed the law ? Have you attended church regularly ; paid your rates and taxes to Cæsar , and contributed, in reason, to charitable institutions? It may be hard to do all these things ; but it is still harder not to do them, as our ninety-nine moral cowards in the hundred well know. And even a scoundrel can do them all and yet live a worse life than the smuggler or prostitute who must answer No all through the catechism. Substitute for such a technical examination one in which the whole point to be settled is, Guilty or Not Guilty ?—one in which there is no more and no less respect for chastity than for incontinence, for subordination than for rebellion, for legality than for illegality, for piety than for blasphemy, in short, for the standard virtues than for the standard vices, and immediately, instead of lowering the moral standard by relaxing the tests of worth, you raise it by increasing their stringency to a point at which no mere Pharisaism or moral cowardice can pass them. Naturally this does not please the Pharisee. The respectable lady of the strictest Christian principles, who has brought up her children with such relentless regard to their ideal morality that if they have any spirit left in them by the time they arrive at years of independence they use their liberty to rush deliriously to the devil—this unimpeachable woman has always felt it unjust that the respect she wins should be accompanied by deep-seated detestation, whilst the latest spiritual heiress of Nell Gwynne, whom no respectable person dare bow to in the street, is a popular idol. The reason is—though the virtuous lady does not know it—that Nell Gwynne is a better woman than she; and the abolition of the idealist test which brings her out a worse one, and its replacement by the realist test which would shew the true relation between them, would be a most desirable step forward in public morals, especially as it would act impartially, and set the good side of the Pharisee above the bad side of the Bohemian as ruthlessly as it would set the good side of the Bohemian above the bad side of the Pharisee. For as long as convention goes counter to reality in these matters, people will be led into Hedda Gabler's error of making an ideal of vice. If we maintain the convention that the distinction between Catherine of Russia and Queen Victoria, between Nell Gwynne and Mrs Proudie, is the distinction between a bad woman and a good woman, we need not be surprised when those who sympathize with Catherine and Nell conclude that it is better to be a bad woman than a good one, and go on recklessly to conceive a prejudice against teetotallism and monogamy, and a prepossession in favour of alcoholic excitement and promiscuous amours. Ibsen himself is kinder to the man who has gone his own way as a rake and a drunkard than to the man who is respectable because he dare not be otherwise. We find that the franker and healthier a boy is, the more certain is he to prefer pirates and highwaymen, or Dumas musketeers, to "pillars of society" as his favourite heroes of romance. We have already seen both Ibsenites and anti-Ibsenites who seem to think that the cases of Nora and Mrs Elvsted are meant to establish a golden rule for women who wish to be "emancipated," the said golden rule being simply, Run away from your husband. But in Ibsen's view of life, that would come under the same condemnation as the conventional golden rule, Cleave to your husband until death do you part. Most people know of a case or two in which it would be wise for a wife to follow the example of Nora or even of Mrs Elvsted. But they must also know cases in which the results of such a course would be as tragi-comic as those of Gregers Werle's attempt in *The Wild Duck* to do for the Ekdal household what Lona Hessel did for the Bernick household. What Ibsen insists on is that there is no golden rule—that conduct must justify itself by its effect upon happiness and not by its conformity to any rule or ideal. And since happiness consists in the fulfilment of the will, which is constantly growing, and cannot be fulfilled to-day under the conditions which secured its fulfilment yesterday, he claims afresh the old Protestant right of private judgment in questions of conduct as against all institutions, the so-called Protestant Churches themselves included.

Here I must leave the matter, merely reminding those who may think that I have forgotten to reduce Ibsenism to a formula for them, that its quintessence is that there is no formula.

APPENDIX.

I HAVE a word or two to add as to the difficulties which Ibsen's philosophy places in the way of those who are called on to impersonate his characters on the stage in England. His idealist figures, at once higher and more mischievous than ordinary Philistines, puzzle by their dual aspect the conventional actor, who persists in assuming that if he is to be selfish on the stage he must be villainous; that if he is to be self-sacrificing and scrupulous he must be a hero; and that if he is to satirize himself unconsciously he must be comic. He is constantly striving to get back to familiar ground by reducing his part to one of the stage types with which he is familiar, and which he has learnt to present by rule of thumb. The more experienced he is, the more certain is he to de-Ibsenize the play into a melodrama or a farcical comedy of the common sort. Give him Helmer to play, and he begins by declaring that the part is a mass of "inconsistencies", and ends by suddenly grasping the idea that it is only Joseph Surface over again. Give him Gregers Werle, the devotee of Truth, and he will first play him in the vein of George

Washington, and then, when he finds that the audience laughs at him instead of taking him respectfully, rush to the conclusion that Gregers is only his old friend the truthful milkman in *A Phenomenon in a Smock Frock*, and begin to play for the laughs and relish them. That is, if there are only laughs enough to make the part completely comic. Otherwise he will want to omit the passages which provoke them. To be laughed at when playing a serious part is hard upon an actor, and still more upon an actress: it is derision, than which nothing is more terrible to those whose livelihood depends on public approbation, and whose calling produces an abnormal development of self-consciousness. Now Ibsen undoubtedly does freely require from his artists that they shall not only possess great skill and power on every plane of their art, but that they shall also be ready to make themselves acutely ridiculous sometimes at the very climax of their most deeply felt passages. It is not to be wondered at that they prefer to pick and choose among the lines of their parts, retaining the great professional opportunities afforded by the tragic scenes, and leaving out the touches which complete the portrait at the expense of the model's vanity. If an actress of established reputation were asked to play Hedda Gabler, her first impulse would

Appendix

probably be to not only turn Hedda into a Brinvilliers, or a Borgia, or a " Forget-me-not ", but to suppress all the meaner callosities and odiousnesses which detract from Hedda's dignity as dignity is estimated on the stage The result would be about as satisfactory to a skilled critic as that of the retouching which has made shop window photography the most worthless of the arts. The whole point of an Ibsen play lies in the exposure of the very conventions upon which are based those by which the actor is ridden. Charles Surface or Tom Jones may be very effectively played by artists who fully accept the morality professed by Joseph Surface and Blifil. Neither Fielding nor Sheridan forces upon either actor or audience the dilemma that since Charles and Tom are lovable, there must be something hopelessly inadequate in the commercial and sexual morality which condemns them as a pair of blackguards The ordinary actor will tell you that the authors "do not defend their heroes' conduct ', not seeing that making them lovable is the most complete defence of their conduct that could possibly be made How far Fielding and Sheridan saw it—how far Molière or Mozart were convinced that the statue had right on his side when he threw Don Juan into the bottomless pit —how far Milton went in his sympathy with Lucifer: all these are speculative points which no actor has hitherto been called upon to solve. But they are the very subjects of Ibsen's plays: those whose interest and curiosity are not excited by them find him the most puzzling and tedious of dramatists. He has not only made "lost" women lovable; but he has recognized and avowed that this is a vital justification for them, and has accordingly explicitly argued on their side and awarded them the sympathy which poetic justice grants only to the righteous. He has made the terms "lost" and "ruined" in this sense ridiculous by making women apply them to men with the most ludicrous effect. Hence Ibsen cannot be played from the conventional point of view: to make that practicable the plays would have to be rewritten. In the rewriting, the fascination of the parts would vanish, and with it their attraction for the performers. *A Doll's House* was adapted in this fashion, though not at the instigation of an actress; but the adaptation fortunately failed. Otherwise we might have to endure in Ibsen's case what we have already endured in that of Shakespear, many of whose plays were supplanted for centuries by incredibly debased versions, of which Cibber's *Richard III.* and Garrick's *Katharine and Petruchio* have lasted to our own time.

Taking Talma's estimate of eighteen years as the apprenticeship of a completely accomplished stage artist, there is little encouragement to offer Ibsen parts to our finished actors and actresses. They do not understand them, and would not play them in their integrity if they could be induced to attempt them. In England only two women in the full maturity of their talent have hitherto meddled with Ibsen. One of these, Miss Geneviève Ward, who "created" the part of Lona Hessel in the English version of *Pillars of Society*, had the advantage of exceptional enterprise and intelligence, and of a more varied culture and experience of life and art than are common in her profession. The other, Mrs Theodore Wright, the first English Mrs Alving, was hardly known to the dramatic critics, though her personality and her artistic talent as an amateur reciter and actress had been familiar to the members of most of the advanced social and political bodies in London since the days of the International. It was precisely because her record lay outside the beaten track of newspaper criticism that she was qualified to surprise its writers as she did. In every other instance, the women who first ventured upon playing Ibsen heroines were young actresses whose ability had not before been fully tested and whose technical apprenticeships were far from complete. Miss Janet Achurch, though she settled the then disputed question of the feasibility of Ibsen's plays on the English stage by her impersonation of Nora in 1889, which still remains the most complete artistic achievement in the new *genre*, had not been long enough on the stage to secure a unanimous admission of her genius, though it was of the most irresistible and irrepressible kind. Miss Florence Farr, who may claim the palm for artistic courage and intellectual conviction in selecting for her experiment *Rosmersholm*, incomparably the most difficult and dangerous, as it is also the greatest, of Ibsen's later plays, had almost relinquished her profession from lack of interest in its routine, after spending a few years in acting farcical comedies. Miss Elizabeth Robins and Miss Marion Lea, to whose unaided enterprise we owe our early acquaintance with *Hedda Gabler* on the stage, were, like Miss Achurch and Miss Farr, juniors in their profession. All four were products of the modern movement for the higher education of women, literate, in touch with advanced thought, and coming by natural predilection on the stage from outside the theatrical class, in contradistinction to the senior generation of inveterately sentimental actresses, schooled in the old fashion if at all, born into their profession, quite out of the political and social movement around them—in short, intellectually *naive* to the last degree. The new school says to the old, You cannot play Ibsen because you are ignoramuses To which the old school retorts, You cannot play anything because you are amateurs. But taking amateur in its sense of unpractised executant, both schools are amateur as far as Ibsen's plays are concerned. The old technique breaks down in the new theatre, for though in theory it is a technique of general application, making the artist so plastic that he can mould himself to any shape designed by the dramatist, in practice it is but a stock of tones and attitudes out of which, by appropriate selection and combination, a certain limited number of conventional stage figures can be made up. It is no more possible to get an Ibsen character out of it than to contrive a Greek costume out of an English wardrobe; and some of the attempts already made have been so grotesque, that at present, when one of the more specifically Ibsenian parts has to be filled, it is actually safer to entrust it to a novice than to a competent and experienced actor.

A steady improvement may be expected in the performances of Ibsen's plays as the young players whom they interest gain the experience needed to make mature artists of them They will gain this experience not only in plays by Ibsen himself, but in the works of dramatists who will have been largely influenced by Ibsen. Playwrights who formerly only compounded plays according to the received prescriptions for producing tears or laughter, are already taking their profession seriously to the full extent of their capacity, and venturing more and more to substitute the incidents and catastrophes of spiritual history for the swoons, surprises, discoveries, murders, duels, assassinations and intrigues which are the commonplaces of the theatre at present. Others, who have no such impulse, find themselves forced to raise the quality of their work by the fact that even those who witness Ibsen's plays with undisguised weariness and aversion, find, when they return to their accustomed theatrical fare, that they have suddenly become conscious of absurdities and artificialities in it which never troubled them before. In just the same way the painters of the Naturalist school reformed their opponents much more extensively than the number of their own direct admirers indicates: for example, it is still common to hear the most contemptuous abuse and ridicule of Monet and Whistler from persons who have nevertheless had their former tolerance of the unrealities of the worst type of conventional studio picture wholly destroyed by these painters Until quite lately, too, musicians were to be heard extolling Donizetti in the same breath with which they vehemently decried Wagner They would make wry faces at every chord in *Tristan und Isolde*, and never suspected that their old faith was shaken until they went back to *La Favorite*, and found that it had become as obsolete as the rhymed tragedies of Lee and Otway. In the drama then, we may depend on it that though we shall not have another Ibsen, yet nobody will write for the stage after him as most playwrights wrote before him. This will involve a corresponding change in the technical stock-in-trade of the actor, whose ordinary training will then cease to be a positive disadvantage to him when he is entrusted with an Ibsen part.

No one need fear on this account that Ibsen will gradually destroy melodrama. It might as well be assumed that Shakespear will destroy music hall entertainments, or the prose romances of William Morris supersede the *Illustrated Police News*. All forms of art rise with the culture and capacity of the human race ; but the forms rise together · the higher forms do not return upon and submerge the lower. The wretch who finds his happiness in setting a leash of greyhounds on a hare or in watching a terrier killing rats in a pit, may evolve into the mere blockhead who would rather go to a " free-and-easy" and chuckle over a dull, silly, obscene song; but such a step will not raise him to the level of the frequenter of music halls of the better class, where, though the entertainment is administered in small separate doses or "turns", yet the turns have some artistic pretension Above him again is the patron of that elementary form of sensational drama in which there is hardly any more connection between the incidents than the fact that the same people take part in them and call forth some very simple sort of moral judgment by being consistently villainous or virtuous throughout. As such a drama would be almost as enjoyable if the acts were played in the reverse of their appointed order, no inconvenience except that of a back seat is suffered by the playgoer who comes in for half price at nine o'clock. On a higher plane we have dramas with a rational sequence of incidents, the interest of any one of which depends on those which have preceded it; and as we go up from plane to plane we find this sequence becoming more and more organic until at last we come to a class of play in which nobody can understand the last act who has not seen the first also. Accordingly, the institution of half price at nine o'clock does not exist at theatres devoted to plays of this class. The highest type of play is completely homogeneous often consisting of a single very complex incident ; and not even the most exhaustive information as to the story enables a spectator to receive the full force of the impression aimed at in any given passage if he enters the theatre for that passage alone. The success of such plays depends upon the exercise by the audience of powers of memory, imagination, insight, reasoning, and sympathy, which only a small minority of the playgoing public at present possesses. To the rest the higher drama is as disagreeably perplexing as the game of chess is to a man who has barely enough capacity to understand skittles. Consequently, just as we have the chess club and the skittle alley prospering side by side, we shall have the theatre of Shakespear, Molière, Goethe, and Ibsen prospering alongside that of Henry Arthur Jones and Gilbert; of Sardou, Grundy, and Pinero ; of Buchanan and Ohnet, as naturally as these already prosper alongside that of Pettit and Sims, which again does no more harm to the music halls than the music halls do to the waxworks or even the ratpit, although this last is dropping into the limbo of discarded brutalities by the same progressive movement that has led the intellectual playgoer to discard Sardou and take to Ibsen. It has often been said that political parties progress serpent-wise, the tail being to-day where the head was formerly, yet never overtaking the head. The same figure may be applied to grades of playgoers, with the reminder that this sort of serpent grows at the head and drops off joints of his tail as he glides along. Therefore it is not only inevitable that new theatres should be built for the new first class of playgoers, but that the best of the existing theatres should be gradually converted to their use, even at the cost of ousting, in spite of much angry protest, the old patrons who are being left behind by the movement.

The resistance of the old playgoers to the new plays will be supported by the elder managers, the elder actors, and the elder critics. One manager pities Ibsen for his ignorance of effective play-writing, and declares that he can see exactly what ought to have been done to make a real play of *Hedda Gabler*. His case is parallel to that of Mr Henry Irving, who saw exactly what ought to have been done to make a real play of Goethe's *Faust*, and got Mr Wills to do it. A third manager, repelled and disgusted by Ibsen, condemns *Hedda* as totally deficient in elevating moral sentiment One of the plays which he prefers is Sardou's *La Tosca!* Clearly these three representative gentlemen, all eminent both as actors and managers, will hold by the conventional drama until the commercial success of Ibsen forces them to recognize that in the course

Appendix.

of nature they are falling behind the taste of the day. Mr Thorne, at the Vaudeville Theatre, was the first leading manager who ventured to put a play of Ibsen's into his evening bill, and he did not do so until Miss Elizabeth Robins and Miss Marion Lea had given ten experimental performances at his theatre at their own risk. Mr Charrington and Miss Janet Achurch, who, long before that, staked their capital and reputation on *A Doll's House*, had to take a theatre and go into management themselves for the purpose. The production of *Rosmersholm* was not a managerial enterprise in the ordinary sense at all: it was an experiment made by Miss Farr, who played Rebecca—an experiment, too, which was considerably hampered by the refusal of the London managers to allow members of their companies to take part in the performance In short, the senior division would have nothing to say for themselves in the matter of the one really progressive theatrical movement of their time, but for the fact that Mr W. H. Vernon's effort to obtain a hearing for *Pillars of Society* in 1880 was the occasion of the first appearance of the name of Ibsen on an English playbill.

But it had long been obvious that the want of a playhouse at which the aims of the management should be unconditionally artistic was not likely to be supplied either at our purely commercial theatres or at those governed by actor-managers reigning absolutely over all the other actors, a power which a young man abuses to provide opportunities for himself, and which an older man uses in an old-fashioned way. Mr William Archer, in an article in the *Fortnightly Review*, invited private munificence to endow a National Theatre; and some time later a young Dutchman, Mr J. T. Grein, an enthusiast in theatrical art, came forward with a somewhat similar scheme. Private munificence remained irresponsive—fortunately, one must think, since it was a feature of both plans that the management of the endowed theatre should be handed over to committees of managers and actors of established reputation—in other words, to the very people whose deficiencies have created the whole difficulty. Mr Grein, however, being prepared to take any practicable scheme in hand himself, soon saw the realities of the situation well enough to understand that to wait for the floating of a fashionable Utopian enterprise, with the Prince of Wales as President and a capital of at least £20,000, would be to wait for ever. He accordingly hired a cheap public hall in Tottenham Court Road, and, though his resources fell far short of those with which an ambitious young professional man ventures upon giving a dance, made a bold start by announcing a performance of *Ghosts* to inaugurate "The Independent Theatre" on the lines of the *Théâtre Libre* of Paris. The result was that he received sufficient support both in money and gratuitous professional aid to enable him to give the performance at the Royalty Theatre; and throughout the following week he shared with Ibsen the distinction of being abusively discussed to an extent that must have amply convinced him that his efforts had not passed unheeded. Possibly he may have counted on being handled generously for the sake of his previous services in obtaining some consideration for the contemporary English drama on the continent, even to the extent of bringing about the translation and production in foreign theatres of some of the most popular of our recent plays; but if he had any such hope it was not fulfilled; for he received no quarter whatever. And at present it is clear that unless those who appreciate the service he has rendered to theatrical art in England support him as energetically as his opponents attack him, it will be impossible for him to maintain the performances of the Independent Theatre at the pitch of efficiency and frequency which will be needed if it is to have any wide effect on the taste and seriousness of the playgoing public. One of the most formidable and exasperating obstacles in his way is the detestable censorship exercised by the official licenser of plays, a public nuisance of which it seems impossible to rid ourselves under existing Parliamentary conditions. The licenser has the London theatres at his mercy through his power to revoke their licenses, and he is empowered to exact a fee for reading each play submitted to him, so that his income depends on his allowing no play to be produced without going through that ordeal. As these powers are granted to him in order that he may forbid the performance of plays which would have an injurious effect on public morals, the unfortunate gentleman is bound in honour to try to do his best to keep the stage in the right path—which he of course can set about in no other way than by making it a reflection of his individual views, which are necessarily dictated by his temperament and by the political and pecuniary interests of his class This he does not dare to do · self-mistrust and the fear of public opinion paralyze him whenever either the strong hand or the open mind claims its golden opportunity; and the net result is that indecency and vulgarity are rampant on the London stage, from which flows the dramatic stream that irrigates the whole country; whilst Shelley's *Cenci* tragedy and Ibsen's *Ghosts* are forbidden, and have in fact only been performed once "in private": that is, before audiences of invited non-paying guests. It is now so well understood that only plays of the commonest idealist type can be sure of a license in London, that the novel and not the drama is the form adopted as a matter of course by thoughtful masters of fiction. The merits of the case ought to be too obvious to need restating: it is plain that every argument that supports a censorship of the stage supports with tenfold force a censorship of the press, which is admittedly an abomination. What is wanted is the entire abolition of the censorship and the establishment of Free Art in the sense in which we speak of Free Trade. There is not the slightest ground for protecting theatres against the competition of music halls, or for denying to Mr Grein as a theatrical *entrepreneur* the freedom he would enjoy as a member of a publishing firm. In the absence of a censorship a manager can be prosecuted for an offence against public morals, just as a publisher can. At present, though managers may not touch Shelley or *Ghosts*, they find no difficulty in obtaining official sanction, practically amounting to indemnity, for indecencies from which our uncensured novels are perfectly free. The truth is that the real support of the censorship comes from those Puritans who regard Art as a department of original sin. To them the theatre is an unmixed evil, and every restriction on it a gain to the cause of righteousness. Against them stand those who regard Art in all its forms as a department of religion. The Holy War between the two sides has played a considerable part in the history of England, and is just now being prosecuted with renewed vigour by the Puritans. If their opponents do not display equal energy, it is quite possible that we shall presently have a reformed censorship ten times more odious than the existing one, the very absurdity of which causes it to be exercised with a halfheartedness that prevents the licenser from doing his worst as well as his best. The wise policy for the friends of Art just now is to use the Puritan agitation in order to bring the matter to an issue, and then to make a vigorous effort to secure that the upshot shall be the total abolition of the censorship.

As it is with the actors and managers, so it is with the critics: the supporters of Ibsen are the younger men. In the main, however, the Press follows the managers instead of leading them. The average newspaper dramatic critic is not a Lessing, a Lamb, or a Lewes · there was a time when he was not necessarily even an accustomed playgoer, but simply a member of the reporting or literary staff told off for theatre duty without any question as to his acquaintance with

Appendix. 153

dramatic literature. At present, though the special nature of his function is so far beginning to be recognized that appointments of the kind usually fall now into the hands of inveterate frequenters of the theatre, yet he is still little more than the man who supplies accounts of what takes place in the playhouses just as his colleague supplies accounts of what takes place at the police court — an important difference, however, being that the editor, who generally cares little about Art and knows less, will himself occasionally criticise, or ask one of his best writers to criticise, a remarkable police case, whereas he never dreams of theatrical art as a subject upon which there could be any editorial policy. Sir Edwin Arnold's editorial attack on Ibsen was due to the accidental circumstance that he, like Richelieu, writes verses between whiles. In fact, the "dramatic critic" of a newspaper, in ordinary circumstances, is at his best a good descriptive reporter, and at his worst a mere theatrical newsman. As such he is a person of importance among actors and managers, and of no importance whatever elsewhere. Naturally he frequents the circles in which alone he is made much of; and by the time he has seen so many performances that he has formed some critical standards in spite of himself, he has also enrolled among his personal acquaintances every actor and manager of a few years' standing, and become engaged in all the private likes and dislikes, the quarrels and friendships, in a word, in all the partialities which personal relations involve, at which point the value of his verdicts may be imagined. Add to this that if he has the misfortune to be attached to a paper to which theatrical advertisements are an object, or of which the editor and proprietors (or their wives) do not hesitate to incur obligations to managers by asking for complimentary admissions, he may often have to choose between making himself agreeable and forfeiting his post. So that he is not always to be relied on even as a newsman where the plain truth would give offence to any individual.

Behind all the suppressive forces with which the critic has to contend comes the law of libel. Every adverse criticism of a public performer is a libel; and any agreement among the critics to boycott artists who appeal to the law is a conspiracy. Of course the boycott does take place to a certain extent; for if an artist, manager, or agent shews any disposition to retort to what is called a "slating" by a lawyer's letter, the critic, who cannot for his own sake expose his employers to the expenses of an action or the anxiety attending the threat of one, will be tempted to shun the danger by simply never again referring to the litigiously disposed person. But although this at first sight seems to sufficiently guarantee the freedom of criticism (for most public persons would suffer more from being ignored by the papers than from being attacked in them, however abusively) its operation is really restricted on the one side to the comparatively few and powerful critics who are attached to important papers at a fixed salary, and on the other to those *entrepreneurs* and artists about whom the public is not imperatively curious. Most critics get paid for their notices at so much per column or per line, so that their incomes depend on the quantity they write. Under these conditions they fine themselves every time they ignore a performance. Again, a dramatist or a manager may attain such a position that his enterprises form an indispensable part of the news of the day. He can then safely intimidate a hostile critic by a threat of legal proceedings, knowing that the paper can afford neither to brave nor ignore him. The late Charles Reade, for example, was a most dangerous man to criticize adversely; but the very writers against whom he took actions found it impossible to boycott him; and what Reade did out of a natural overflow of indignant pugnacity, some of our more powerful artistic *entrepreneurs* occasionally threaten to do now after a deliberate calculation of the advantages of their position. If legal proceedings are actually taken, and the case is not, as usual, compromised behind the scenes, the uncertainty of the law receives its most extravagant illustration from a couple of lawyers arguing a question of fine art before a jury of men of business. Even if the critic were a capable speaker and pleader, which he is not in the least likely to be, he would be debarred from conducting his own case by the fact that his comparatively wealthy employer and not himself would be the defendant in the case. In short, the law is against straightforward criticism at the very points where it is most needed; and though it is true that an ingenious and witty writer can make any artist or performance acutely ridiculous in the eyes of ingenious and witty people without laying himself open to an action, and indeed with every appearance of good-humoured indulgence, such applications of wit and ingenuity do criticism no good; whilst in any case they offer no remedy to the plain critic writing for plain readers.

All this does not mean that the entire Press is hopelessly corrupt in its criticism of Art. But it certainly does mean that the odds against the independence of the Press critic are so heavy that no man can maintain it completely without a force of character and a personal authority which are rare in any profession, and which in most of them can command higher pecuniary terms and prospects than any which journalism can offer. The final degrees of thoroughness have no market value on the Press, for, other things being equal, a journal with a critic who is goodhumoured and compliant will have no fewer readers than one with a critic who is inflexible where the interests of Art and the public are concerned. I do not exaggerate or go beyond the warrant of my own experience when I say that unless a critic is prepared not only to do much more work than the public will pay him for, but to risk his livelihood every time he strikes a serious blow at the powerful interests vested in artistic abuses of all kinds (conditions which in the long run tire out the strongest man), he must submit to compromises which detract very considerably from the trustworthiness of his criticism. Even the critic who is himself in a position to brave these risks must find a sympathetic and courageous editor-proprietor who will stand by him without reference to the commercial advantage—or disadvantage—of his incessant warfare. As all the economic conditions of our society tend to throw our journals more and more into the hands of successful moneymakers, the exceeding scarcity of this lucky combination of resolute, capable, and incorruptible critic, sympathetic editor, and disinterested and courageous proprietor, can hardly be appreciated by those who only know the world of journalism through its black and white veil.

On the whole, though excellent criticisms are written every week by men who, either as writers distinguished in other branches of literature and journalism, or as civil servants, are practically independent of this or that particular appointment as dramatic critic (not to mention the few whom strong vocation and force of character have rendered incorruptible) there remains a great mass of newspaper reports of theatrical events which is only called dramatic criticism by courtesy. Among the critics properly so called opinions are divided about Ibsen in the inevitable way into Philistine, idealist, and realist (more or less). Just at present the cross firing between them is rather confusing. Without being necessarily an Ibsenist, a critic may see at a glance that abuse of the sort quoted on page 89 is worthless; and he may for the credit of his cloth attack it on that ground. Thus we have Mr A. B. Walkley, of *The Speaker*, one of the most able and independent of our critics, provoking Mr Clement Scott beyond measure by alluding to the writers who had just been calling the admirers of Ibsen "muck-ferreting dogs", as "these gentry", with a good-humoured but very perceptible contempt for their literary attainments. Thereupon Mr Scott publishes a vindication of the literateness of that school, of which Mr Walkley makes unmerciful fun. But Mr Walkley is by no means committed to Ibsenism by his appreciation of Ibsen's status as an artist, much less by his depreciation of the literary status of Ibsen's foes. On the other hand there is Mr Frederick Wedmore, a professed admirer of Balzac, conceiving such a violent antipathy to Ibsen that he almost echoes Sir Edwin Arnold, whose denunciations are at least as applicable to the author of *Vautrin* as to the author of *Ghosts*. Mr George Moore, accustomed to fight on behalf of Zola against the men who are now attacking Ibsen, takes the field promptly against his old enemies in defence, not of Ibsenism, but of Free Art. Even Mr William Archer expressly guards himself against being taken as an Ibsenist doctrinaire. In the face of all this, it is little to the point that some of the critics who have attacked Ibsen have undoubtedly done so because—to put it bluntly— they are too illiterate and incompetent in the sphere of dramatic poetry to conceive or relish anything more substantial than the theatrical fare to which they are accustomed; or that others, intimidated by the outcry raised by Sir

Edwin Arnold and the section of the public typified by Pastor Manders (not to mention Mr Pecksniff), against their own conviction join the chorus of disparagement from modesty, caution, compliance — in short, from want of the courage of their profession. There is no reason to suppose that if the whole body of critics had been endowed with a liberal education and an independent income, the number of Ibsenists among them would be much greater than at present, however the tone of their adverse criticism might have been improved Ibsen, as a pioneer in stage progress no less than in morals, is bound to have the majority of his contemporaries against him, whether as actors, managers, or critics.

Finally, it is necessary to say, by way of warning, that many of the minor combatants on both sides have either not studied the plays at all, or else have been so puzzled that they have allowed themselves to be misled by the attacks of the idealists into reading extravagant immoralities between the lines, as, for instance, that Oswald in *Ghosts* is really the son of Pastor Manders, or that Lövborg is the father of Hedda Tesman's child. It has even been asserted that horrible exhibitions of death and disease occur in almost every scene of Ibsen's plays, which, for tragedies, are exceptionally free from visible physical horrors. It is not too much to say that very few of the critics have yet got so far as to be able to narrate accurately the stories of the plays they have witnessed. No wonder, then, that they have not yet made up their minds on the more difficult point of Ibsen's philosophic drift—though I do not myself see how performances of his plays can be quite adequately judged without reference to it. One consequence of this is that those who are interested, fascinated, and refreshed by Ibsen's art misrepresent his meaning benevolently quite as often as those who are perplexed and disgusted misrepresent it maliciously; and it already looks as if Ibsen might attain undisputed supremacy as a modern playwright without necessarily converting a single critic to Ibsenism. Indeed it is not possible that his meaning should be fully recognized, much less assented to, until Society as we now know it loses its self-complacency through the growth of the conviction foretold by Richard Wagner when he declared that "Man will never be that which he can and should be until, by a conscious following of that inner natural necessity which is the only true necessity, he makes his life a mirror of nature, and frees himself from his thraldom to outer artificial counterfeits. Then will he first become a living man, who now is a mere wheel in the mechanism of this or that Religion, Nationality, or State."

BIBLIOLIFE

Old Books Deserve a New Life
www.bibliolife.com

Did you know that you can get most of our titles in our trademark **EasyScript**[TM] print format? **EasyScript**[TM] provides readers with a larger than average typeface, for a reading experience that's easier on the eyes.

Did you know that we have an ever-growing collection of books in many languages?

Order online:
www.bibliolife.com/store

Or to exclusively browse our **EasyScript**[TM] collection:
www.bibliogrande.com

At BiblioLife, we aim to make knowledge more accessible by making thousands of titles available to you – quickly and affordably.

Contact us:
BiblioLife
PO Box 21206
Charleston, SC 29413

Lightning Source UK Ltd.
Milton Keynes UK
07 September 2010

159523UK00006B/3/P